PRAISE FOR B2B A

" We're in the middle of a communications revolution with an explosion of new media channels, including social networks, to reach your buyers directly. But most B2B companies act as if we're still in the 1950s. This is not your grandfather's era. If you want to grow your business, you need to adopt the strategies Bill outlines in this book."

David Meerman Scott,
bestselling author of *The New Rules of Marketing and PR*,
now in over 25 languages from Bulgarian to Vietnamese.

" It was written in the stars that a man named Bill Blaney would write the best B2B marketing book ever!"

George Lois,
advertising legend and author of eight books,
including *Damn Good Advice (For People With Talent!)*

" Blaney does a fantastic job of synthesizing traditional and digital marketing tactics and strategies and making them relevant for B2B marketers. He speaks the B2B management language. If you're a marketing manager for a manufacturer or a consultant who provides marketing services to B2B businesses, you will find this a fantastic resource because Blaney describes everything in simple, yet complete language that your clients and leadership will understand and buy into... I wish I had written this book. It is thorough and includes just about every critical topic B2B businesses need to be successful without being overwhelming and leaving you with the feeling that you will never be able to accomplish this."

Ivana Taylor,
Small Business Trends

" 4 1/2 out of 5 stars! I really enjoyed reading this book and bet you will to. Bill pulls no punches and tells it like it is."

Jeff Ogden,
Marketing Made Simple TV

" It's a changed business environment for most companies these days. This book offers vitally important information for B2B'ers."

Patricia Faulhaber,
Blogcritics

B2B A TO Z

Marketing tools and strategies that generate
leads for your Business-to-Business company

Bill Blaney

DENHAM PUBLISHING, INC.

Published by Denham Publishing, Inc.

ISBN 978-0-9884977-0-2 (Paperback)

ISBN 978-0-9884977-1-9 (Hardcover)

ISBN 978-0-9884977-2-6 (eBook)

For Aya, Billy and Ashlyn

For my parents.

Also dedicated to Jim Overend,
one of the best marketing men I've had
the honor of working with.

TABLE OF CONTENTS

Introduction

I have a daughter. She has an uncommon name. Not unique, but uncommon. As a result, there is nothing harder than trying to find a cup, or pendant, or bracelet with her name on it. We search through custom product displays at specialty stores in hopes that some company somewhere would recognize that our daughter's name exists. So far we've come up empty handed – or have had to settle for items with a name similar to hers. *Justin? Emma? Will?* Sure, they are all represented well in the name-branded item category. They're the well-known names, like Apple, IBM and Amazon. There's always something made to identify with them.

How about you? Do you have a similar problem as it relates to your business research? Is your category unique but not uncommon? When you look for, say, a book on a subject that relates to it are you finding what you need—or are you settling for one that sounds similar but only really talks to Justin, Emma and Will?

You've probably picked up this book because you're a business person looking to learn more about business-to-business (B2B) marketing, an advertising or digital agency leader who wants to stay current with what's going on, a business owner looking to make more, or a digital strategist or B2B marketing manager trying to succeed better at what you do. You've probably also spent a good deal of time searching for books or guides that address your line or work – a business that sells to other businesses. Chances are you've had little luck finding them or, when you have, they've left you with very little to chew on. There really isn't that much out there for you, but I'm hoping to change that right here between these covers.

The truth of the matter is that B2B marketing has always been the Jan Brady to consumer marketing's Marcia. It has never received the respect (or attention) that consumer does; it's misunderstood by the masses (and sometimes, even by clients); and it has so few written resources to help its practitioners that it's only natural that companies are behind the curve on new developments in the field. The cry for help is understood: we simply want to know what to do, what to avoid, and what actually works. It's a difficult thing to do given that companies are as different as apples and oranges. Nonetheless, you would figure someone out there would be able to cull together enough universal truths about B2B marketing to create some type of "bible" on success in the industry.

Some of the changes in this industry have come so fast and hard that business heads are swimming. Social, mobile, experiential…but it's not just new words every marketing manager and strategist needs to learn but their complex functions and how to manipulate them to actually affect a company's bottom line. It also doesn't help that most of the recent case studies of success, particularly in the social space, are usually documented about well-known institutional outfits that have gargantuan marketing budgets, like a Dell or a Cisco. While the success of a campaign that has included a well-placed series of expensive commercials (which you don't find in B2B) and a media blitz to rival Paris Hilton is nice for those companies, those success stories hardly matter to a company that sells shipping supplies, computer components, or food additives to partner companies that use them. They are a less-than-effective measure of how a manufacturer with a $20,000 - $800,000 marketing budget can spread that money out in all the places it's expected to hit.

I've been on the agency side of the marketing business for my entire career, and I've been involved in B2B for the last 12 years. My clients have included Canon, Capital One Bank, Showtime, JP Morgan Chase, Clear Channel, Department Of Veterans Affairs, Colgate-Palmolive, and many others, large and small. I've played my part in creating media for NBC Olympics, introducing new products to the market for Canon, Konica Minolta and Chase Small Business, and training startups on what's available to them and how to properly go to market with their products and services. I've developed wide-reaching campaigns and unique promotions with some of the best people in the industry and I've made the point of learning from them. I've been a Creative Director, Copywriter, Marketing Strategist, Digital Expert, Social Media Guru and New Business point person at different times in my career and, many times, all things at once. I've also been actively involved in the digital space since 1995, creating online and interactive campaigns for clients since that time. The first social marketing campaign I worked on was developed in 2001, long before the term "social marketing" was part of the general vernacular. Even as a kid, I had a dad in the industry—an original "Mad Man" who held creative positions at McCann, Grey, and many others along the way.

When you've been in the trenches as long as I have, you learn pretty quickly what formulas and strategies lead to success and what to avoid. I'm happy to pass along these insights to you as well as some other successful B2B strategies that continue to reap dividends. (Having actual data that they've done so is also helpful, and I've got that, too). I also wanted to write a book that the reader can use as needed. Want to learn tools and strategies? There are chapters for that. Want to understand the B2B market better? Read those chapters first. Business books should work like good marketing materials – you should be able to learn what you need to learn without listening to the whole album first. And if you want to go from the first to the last page in that order it's built for you, too.

In addition, my extended hope was to be honest and truthful with you about what you can expect from all this new noise. Just because someone tells you to start a blog doesn't mean it's right for your company. Just because it's standard to pay for a Facebook page as part of a social marketing campaign doesn't guarantee your customers will ever contact you through it. Just because you get your content out there to your audience doesn't mean it will be read by them unless you do more to get eyes on it. None of this should discourage you, though. There are very effective ways to leverage your brand in the B2B marketplace and come out on top.

Will anyone in my industry be angry that I'm giving away the farm, opening up the curtain, or slaying a few sacred cows? I can't see why. Ten years from now, there will be another book describing all the new media channels that we can't even conceive of now. Everyone will be absorbing content through their sunglasses or some other new device. Strategies to get traffic through websites like SEO will be dramatically different because the programming language used to create these sites (if they are even called "sites" then) will be different. Some new form of media may crop up and blow all of our current media darlings out of the water. To quote Bill Murray from the movie "Meatballs": *"It just doesn't matter."* What does matter is sharing what is learned so others can take it and run with it. What does matter is letting marketers understand what is possible for their budgets despite what a bloated agency with million-dollar offices to maintain might be telling them. What does matter is that you, the marketing professional, get what you pay for, understand that not *everything* spent in an advertising budget is about ROI or should be, and that someone with the title "Director of Digital Strategy" isn't all that alien from you and your position.

So here it is, soup to nuts. B2B A to Z. To you from me.

Bill Blaney

CHAPTER 1:

B2B Marketing Has Changed

Successful businesses are like amoebas: they move, morph, split, and change in order to grow. Being "amoeba-like" keeps these businesses ahead of the curve in an economy that has become trans-global, hyper-competitive, and dramatically more complex than the business world we knew even five years ago. As we strive to adapt to this new 24-hour/100-mile-a-minute lifestyle, smart businesses have learned that upward momentum and increasing profits reside not only in the strength of a company's products or services (or the forward-thinking attitude of its employer and employees), but in the clarity and impact of its marketing.

To succeed in today's business environment, you must

market; but to market in this new environment, you must change. Success is about more than creating a blog or a website, folks. It's about redefining your marketing strategy and how it will evolve. It's not as simple as starting a Facebook page or a Twitter account, but it's also not as complex as you might think it is. It's really about using the right combination of tools—social, digital, visual, experiential, and, yes, even print—in a way that helps your company thrive. It's also about looking beyond what your competition is currently doing. In the case of B2B marketing, change tends to happen more slowly, while the pace of the business productivity and innovation increases. For those companies who understand that this new world order is an alarm bell to reassess their own marketing strategies, more power to you. There's a lot to do in the short term, and I hope my input here will be a helpful step in that direction.

Traditional Media's Reach Has Diminished

In a study released last year, Google surveyed 600 business-to-business marketing professionals in late 2010. It asked them questions about how they planned to spend their marketing budget in the upcoming year, the effectiveness of previous programs, and the challenges ahead. It wasn't surprising that most marketing budgets favored trade shows, print ads, direct mail, and other forms of "traditional" media 62% over online and social. Old was winning out over new.

In reality, the larger truth in this survey is that many B2B advertisers (especially small and medium-sized businesses) are slow to adapt to new ways of marketing, even when the trade shows they attend have become less populated and the publications they've spent years advertising in have shrunk to half the size. Sure, there are still gains to be had by handing out a flyer or trinket to your trade show booth visitor, but it's more likely your potential customer will visit you on the web or search for your services in Google first. As we know all too well—as evidenced in the technological shift to hand-held devices, online news sources, and digital social interactions—today's customer views business-related material differently. For business, this has meant that the small prisms of professional and vetted sources that have been so reliable in years past (direct mail, print, email, and those ever-dwindling trade shows) are only one part of the equation today. Most information that finds our clients today comes from an endless, ever-increasing variety of new media channels. As a result, clients make up their minds about products, services, and events in a more fluid manner than ever before. We've become inundated. And whereas in earlier generations, popular culture (and our limited, more controlled arteries of information) influenced us more than we influenced it, that dynamic has flipped.

Advertising clutter has increased, and many have been turned off—but for countless others the perception is changing. With mobile devices and smart pads, advertisers have found ways to make banner ads and rich-media marketing work. Customers have become part of the clutter as well as self-designated media critics and promoters. As a result, the dividing line between work related activity and recreational is no longer well defined anymore—and a seasoned product reviewer can be just as influential as a novice. Media and the public are no longer two sides of a spectrum anymore. They swim in the same waters. Marketers need to take notice and adjust accordingly.

Media's Influence Changes For Each Generation

Addressing the electronically connected generation is something every company should be adjusting to right now. As someone who grew up in the late 1970s / early 1980s but has always been a digital junkie, I've had the opportunity to observe at large (and particularly through my digitally-savvy industry) how media has completely changed the communication landscape. Every generation, it appears, has taken its part. For example, baby boomers spent more hours away from media. Television was relegated to a few shows per week that were looked forward to and excitedly discussed. Education about the world at large came from parents, our teachers, the Encyclopaedia Britannica, the World Book Encyclopedia, and whatever stood out at the local library. Advertising's ability to embed itself into their lives was measured.

The generation that followed—Generation X (my generation)—had a slightly different experience. TV provided abundant choices, our mailboxes were suddenly filled with bulky yet colorful promotions, counter cards sat at every local business, and a host of niche magazines surfaced on every subject and for every interest.

And how has the latest generation's experience contrasted with that? Whew! Where do we start? We've moved from modest invasions in our private lives with beepers in the early '90s to the expectation that people can—and should—be accessible anywhere and at any time. Advertising is not so much intrusive as it is ingrained, from the product placement in an Adam Sandler film to the sidebar on our Facebook profiles to the banner ad at the bottom of our iPhone game. Whether at work or at play, we absorb far more than we can possibly process. The real world and the virtual world have merged. Even in exercises such as driving, our attention isn't always focused on the task at hand: some of us may be on the phone, texting, or taking furtive glances at Facebook while at red lights or during long stretches. It's a surprise more accidents don't occur as a result of such cluttered and busy minds.

Thanks to this uncontrolled media saturation, people have become more aggressive gatekeepers of what is inevitably allowed to seep in. When a stimulus fails to grab our attention immediately, it has little chance of ever doing it. In response to this dynamic, marketing campaigns have matured greatly. The industry today has more complex and multifaceted strategies to accommodate multiple customer categories and respond to purchases based on unique and particular needs.

New Media's Altered The Landscape. Just Look At The Music Industry

No industry embodies the dramatic change our digital and social landscape has brought us more than the music industry. Less than 15 years ago, consumers visited record stores and purchased CDs. Radio was the principal mover of what was popular, and those choices were made largely by disc jockeys (with help from powerful music companies who had their ear). Word of mouth was certainly important, but the key shaper of what the public listened to had little to do with blog comments from the average Joe. Popular culture was crafted behind closed doors and without our help. Executives decided who the next big thing would be and promoted them as such. Unless that celebrity or band was a miserable mess, they made some of the numbers that were expected of them. This was the same strategy used in the old Hollywood studio system back in the 1930s, 40s and 50s, where idols were cultivated in house and sold to the public as full-blown stars before anybody other than their parents appreciated them. We were spoon fed rock and roll, bubble gum, and Britney Spears—and we ate it up with few complaints. That was just the way it was.

Today, CDs are history. We no longer think of music in terms of "albums." Radio is still relevant, but its influence has been diminished by the introduction of multiple media sources, including YouTube, blogs, and Pandora. Discovering tomorrow's stars has become an interactive—or, to be specific, "community"—experience, through the success of TV shows like *American Idol* and *X Factor*.

The niche markets in music, which were previously relegated to the back of the line, became the main focus, and the market leaders change daily. It's more akin to professional boxing: there is no longer only one heavyweight champion. Instead, buying your favorite music/movie/clothing/electronic product/furniture/utility has become just like purchasing a beer. The choices are absolutely and profoundly endless, and the locations for purchase are too numerous to count. For some businesses, particularly the consumer-based, this augmentation has been a blessing. Small companies now occupy the same space as institutional ones, and the power of social media has leveled the playing field. Social channels that we currently spend a substantial portion of our time on – Facebook, YouTube, Twitter, etc. – are the perfect vehicles to address people's desires and an ample opportunity for consumers to critique new products and services, particularly those that appeal to them. Furthermore, these new channels are built on a bedrock of entertainment, popular culture, and material wants. In contrast to, say, the purchase of a water-softener product for your employer's industrial steam boiler, most consumers love to discuss their latest buys with friends and to offer their reviews. Brands have become social lubricants. The recommendations we make to friends and acquaintances about which lawn mower to buy and what skateboard manufacturer to seek out has becomes a big part of our online interactions. And this dynamic will continue to grow and mature.

The Challenge for B2B Companies

Here's the real question: Has the development of these new media channels been a benefit for business-to-business companies? Have they been able to capitalize on these one-on-one conversations in the same way, and with a comparable level of success, that a company like Coca-Cola or Apple has? Are their customers as open to conducting business through this method of communication/commerce as, say, a teenager with his or her parents credit card? The answer, sadly, is that it doesn't seem so. As a result of this gap, we find average B2B companies struggling to cope. While the business world has taken ownership of a few social channels (such as LinkedIn and Slideshare), most B2B marketing campaigns have remained conservative and antiquated. Make no mistake: B2B marketing has never been as colorful, connected, and forward-thinking as consumer marketing. That alone would account for why many B2B marketing campaigns are either crashing bores or trying so desperately to be "consumer-styled" that their messages get muddled. And when the vacuum of familiarity appears far less scary and confusing than the latest and newest techniques, most companies find themselves sticking to the "tried and true": ads in trade magazines, direct mail, maybe a banner ad somewhere, and trade show brochures, among other things. Or they decide to forgo anything new altogether by offering up out-of-date marketing materials created years earlier and displaying them at anemic trade-show booths. Can the business-to-business industry catch up? Certainly. We've already begun to.

Marketing Differently Than Before Is The Key

As a B2B marketer with many years in the trenches and

an early adopter of social marketing techniques and rich-media advertising, I still agree with most business leaders that no website, Facebook post, or colorfully phrased email alone can outmatch the power of a one-on-one conversation with a potential lead. But as any good businessperson knows, leads can come from the most unlikely places, and you only need one good one to change your company's life. By the same token, there will always be businesses that never ever benefit or gain leads through social means (at least not in the short term). Like it or not, brand-building through social channels is here to stay, despite its less-than-perfect fit for business customers. In addition, as today's decision-makers exit the workforce and tomorrow's tech-weaned become the next generation of movers and shakers, all businesses will be required to utilize these new tools, like them, and understand them—or not. The smartest path forward is to accept that a mix of new and old marketing techniques, applied correctly, will yield results that guarantee brand survival.

Usually, the best advertising strategies lie not to the extremes of the current norm but somewhere in between - and B2B marketers need to understand that more work is involved to engage their customers today than in years past, particularly when competitors are many. Marketing does work. Sometimes slowly, other times quicker than we're prepared for. What has never worked is sitting still. Do that, and success will most certainly pass you by.

Consumer vs. B2B Marketing: The Difference Between Wants and Needs

I have a colleague of mine who's a Creative Director like me. There was a new account on his roster, and he was anxious about how difficult it might be to concept for this client and even some of his others lately. He explained how complex and layered his consumer campaigns needed to be and how the competition had all the good angles sewn up. He then told me how lucky I was to be working in business-to-business advertising. How much easier it must be to pitch clients who don't expect the kind of humor and nuance he's required to cultivate every single day at work. Was I insulted? No. I've heard this song before. It's a familiar one in advertising circles.

In response, I explained to him that, despite his current dilemma, he was enormously lucky to have the problem of marketing directly to consumers and that B2B, despite his understanding, was as far from a walk in the park as you can get.

To be crystal clear, there is *nothing* easy or nuance-free about B2B marketing compared to B2C. Not one single, solitary thing. And the difference between the two, including the potential difficulty of the sale, can be narrowed down to something as simple as **wants** and **needs**.

Consumer advertising, at its most complex, is always about selling to wants. *I want that dress. I want this car. I want that computer. I want that salad dressing.* Some may argue that there are products that fall into the consumer category that are needs and not wants. For example, some people may believe they *need* a particular lawn mower or vacuum cleaner. They *need* Proactive Solution to remove their pimples, or Just For Men to get rid of their gray. But there is a difference in the sale of these types of items that can't be ignored, and that difference comes down to this:

Can the consumer survive without these products or services?

They may tell you they can't. They may even say they're unable to live without them. But prior to the purchase, these folks were getting along just fine, more or less. Maybe they weren't as satisfied with the vacuum cleaner they had and they recognized the improvements of a Dyson, or maybe their boss mentioned that their appearance in meetings may need a youthful boost and they should think about hair coloring, but the truth is that the exclusion of these items from their lives would not stop them dead in their tracks. In most cases, it would also not cost them tangibly or substantially.

Are there products and services that consumers honestly and truly *need?* Sure. But most things we don't truly need. Our species lived with very little for a very long time before cell phones, purses, or frozen dinners appeared on the scene. As a consumer, the truth is we really just *want* many of these items. Good advertising, and there is some of it out there, can go a long way in convincing someone otherwise, but when you are marketing to a business, the rules of *want* are trumped time and again by the much more stringent rules of *need.*

Needs-Based Marketing: It's Not Flirting, It's Marriage

Businesses *need* certain products and services to stay in business. They need other products and services to grow their business. They need a different variety of products and services to lend an air of personality or success or seriousness to their business that will help brand them in a positive light. In the final equation, however, the bottom line for most business purchases has little to do with wants. Wants are impulses. Needs require a bit more persuasion and a clarity in the purchase that must be addressed. It's the difference between flirting and proposing marriage.

Here's a good example, in very human terms, of the how the sale differs between the two. Remember that girl or guy from high school who barely knew you but you had a terrible crush on? For those of you out there who won over your crushes, how did you convince him or her that you were worthy? Let me take a guess: You probably succeeded by letting them get to know you and, as a result, want you in their lives. To make them want you, you appealed to them through common interests you both identified with, or through humor, or through a subtle (or sometimes not-so-subtle) display of how sexy, strong, or attractive you were. You won them over by appealing to some or all of the things they wanted in a relationship or looked for in a date. For a few of you, it may just have been a case of physical attraction and that was all that was necessary to close the deal. That's the way it rolls sometimes.

Then you start dating. After a while, you become an item. This crush becomes a part of your life. Eventually, over time, you come to the belief that you need that person and can't do without him or her. It didn't happen overnight. It was a process that started with an attraction – and an impulse.

Now, as an exercise, imaging having to sell yourself to a crush – someone who doesn't even have the slightest idea who you are - on the notion that he or she *needs* you. It's a tougher sell, isn't it?

But needs are the barriers that must be crossed in a sale to a business. Businesses don't think in terms of what they have in common with a product or service. They don't necessarily care how sexy or funny that product or service is. What concerns them is the bottom line, and the bottom line is whether the product or service will either A) Increase their profits or B) Make their business more efficient.

Selling To Wants And Needs:
Apple Computer

A good example of a "Want" campaign is Apple's iMac commercials from a few years ago. On one side of the screen, we have "PC": boring, stodgy, and set in his ways. On the other side is the cool, relaxed, artsy, and intelligent Apple guy. Forget about whether you're an Apple or PC person now. On a purely personal level, which guy would you want to be? I'd bet that even the stodgiest, boring, most set-in-their-ways individuals don't see themselves in that light. They envision themselves as being cool and smart. They identify with Apple and they *want* to be identified that way because it says something about them personally. It is the "brand" they want to be associated with.

Human beings are predisposed to personal "branding" as part of our DNA. When young, most of us went through a phase where we needed to be identified as individuals separate from our families. We cultivated the appropriate looks and gravitated toward items, from music to sports to technology, that reinforced this brand, projecting to others who we were or who we wanted to be. Punkers, Goths, Metalheads, Preps, Emos, Jocks... all attempts at branding. Some deliberate, others accidental. We adorned our identities. Clothing. Makeup. Accessories. When I was a kid in 1974, Puma and Adidas sneakers broke through the clutter. Prior to their arrival, everyone I knew wore Pro-Keds. Within the scope of a month or two after a popular classmate showed up in one of these unusual and new sneakers, Pumas and Adidas took over the school. They were a little sleeker. It said something about you that you wore them.

Some kids, I recall, bought sneakers that were knock-offs of those two brands. "He's got skips!" was the popular taunt by those who wanted to be cruel. Skips—that was a spontaneously developed slang for sneakers that didn't fit the social status of Pumas and Adidas. As a result, we all learned early on how identification with a product defined how others viewed us.

Now, how would the Apple/PC campaign have changed if it were pitched to businesses instead of consumers? Would businesses really care whether a computer they purchase is cool or not? No. Do businesses whose offices are mostly out of sight from clients *need* to purchase an Apple computer because it's "cool?" Probably not. Would the change in the campaign address something more substantial than appealing to the desire of the individual purchaser? You bet.

What do we understand that businesses value when it comes to purchasing computers? Performance and memory. Speed and reliability. Service. They are concerned whether all the computer programs that they bought last month will work with these new machines. If not, they'll need to know if the cost-to-profit ratio will justify buying new software. As a result, Apple (along with most companies) cannot appeal to this kind of audience in the same way it can to a consumer audience. In Apple's case, its marketing plan includes a strategy for B2B. If you take a look in any trade magazine or website, Apple's advertising is skewed toward features as opposed to emotions. Apple knows what its business customers need to convince the IT and money people in their companies that an Apple product is the best business choice for them.

One of the smartest moves Apple made early in its history was to partner with companies that produced software for the publishing and design businesses. This was a major benchmark in its B2B strategy. By selling itself as the premiere conduit for users of Photoshop, Quark, Illustrator, PageMaker, InDesign and others—and by advertising within the B2B spaces about Apple's compatibility with these business mainstays—Apple grew to quickly own this desirable market before the competition could even get its bearings. And it managed to do this without being cutesy or flirtatious.

"Needs" Define How B2B Companies Do Business

The *needs* of your client should define exactly what kind of marketing campaign you should develop and the kind you need to avoid. To ignore the difference is to veer markedly off track. Misunderstanding your B2B clients and concluding that sexiness or a little song and dance can win the day is anathema to your business strategy, as much as boring the living hell out of them is. This is not to say flirting in business is not productive. One-on-one relationships between clients and vendors very much involves a mixture of wants and needs. A client/vendor relationship is exactly that—a relationship—and it may require a bit of seduction at the outset. But although some clients may respond to humor and intelligence (and believe that your product or service is everything you say it is), they may still need the facts. On average, the decision-makers at a computer manufacturer aren't going to go with your microchip simply because you play a great game of golf. They have to be convinced they *need* your product. They need to be persuaded that your microchip will make their computers go faster and their processors remain stable. They may want white papers or case studies or testimonials from previous clients or companies. They may need to view a forum where other users are discussing your microchip or where they can find reviews. As you can see, for a business purchase, *want* is

easily squashed by *need*. This holds true whether you're dealing with the owner of a business or a mid-level "buyer." In
short, business customers, particularly employees, have three
concerns when making the decision to buy your product
or service:

1. Will this product help my company?

When employees put on their business hats, they
forgo a certain portion of their own personae to take on that
of their employer. In order to perform their jobs correctly,
employees, managers, and buyers must accept that the good of
the company is their primary focus. In accepting that, their
decisions in making purchases are not tied to their personal
desires but that of their company's needs. Moreover, a
particular purchase has probably been vetted through at least
one previous meeting if not several.

*Sure, we all know people who spend most of their time on
the job feeding their own needs and desires, but those people are
rarely the ones moving companies forward. At some point or
another, if they are any good at what they do, they have to work
for the good of the place giving them a paycheck. Companies
don't perform well when everyone works on their own island.
Larger ones especially.*

2. Will this purchase help me?

According to a study by Enquiro Research, 99% of 3,000
business buyers who were questioned stated that the most B2B
buying decisions are driven by a need to control personal and
organizational risk—in other words, "to cover my ass." Make
no mistake. When it comes to employees, particularly those
at large firms but not to the exclusion of smaller ones, the
subtext of your sale has everything to do with his or her
standing at the company. Every decision made speaks to

their management skills and, for some, these decisions must be tied to a comfort factor that confirms that choosing you will not jeopardize their job. As an ad agency, we like to consider ourselves extensions of our particular contact at a client company. Despite the overall expectation that our work is spectacular and on-target, we also understand that our job is to make our contact look good, predict what he or she might need next even when they don't request it, and reinforce the notion that picking us as the service was a smart move for everyone involved. On the other hand, we've lost business in the past that would normally have gone to us but was forwarded to a much larger and well-known agency. The lesson there was a simple one: no-one is going to get fired for picking BBDO or Deutsch. A client's personal needs at work may not extend to making business-related purchases, but the purchases he does make can personally affect their lives. Therefore, the human psychology of every business relationship cannot be ignored—unless you're dealing with robots.

3. Will this purchase result in extra profits?

Sure. You may be a paper towel distributor to a large restaurant chain, but at the end of the day, this is about two things: Are the towels hardy enough that customers don't have to waste two or three when one should be sufficient? And is the cost of the towel low enough that profit won't be affected elsewhere in the restaurant? Profits, in the end, are everything for your clients. If your product cannot be positioned as a profit center or a necessity for your client, you will have a tough time selling it, no matter what you do. Good marketing is there to make the argument for companies that are unable to tell their story themselves. The connection between your product and their profit is vital.

What Can Happen When No One Listens

Any good agency should be able to make some targeted marketing recommendations to their clients with a moderate level of understanding about how they might play out. If you've done your homework on a company, know who its market is, and understand its customers decision-making criteria, certain communication markers should naturally fall into place. Nonetheless, the final decision about how a company should market itself and whether the need of the B2B customer is being addressed comes down to the knowledge and awareness of its marketing manager. Many are smart individuals who know their audience better than the agency does. Others may lack the experience to quantify the data they're presented with. Still others will travel their own road while ignoring common sense.

We had a client, an information technology company, several years back whose new marketing executive had never worked in the advertising field at all; previously, he had been an administrator in healthcare. The company's product was a service to help patients gather and compile medical information for easy retrieval, but it was months away from completion.

The company's target market was large corporations and educational institutions. Its product was a "value-added" item for health benefits that employees already received. The thinking was that this information-gathering tool (which the company wanted to market for $30 a month) was something employees could use well and businesses could benefit from by making their health packages more attractive.

In researching the market, we came to the conclusion that the target audience—which was health benefit administrators—needed to be convinced that this product would help them in their recruitment efforts, while being of minimal cost to the company. Their decisions were based strongly on the same three benchmarks I discussed in "Wants and Needs." Unfortunately, our client didn't agree or see the company's audience the same way; as a result, the client decided to create their advertising in-house with another selling strategy altogether. It wasn't a result of us being wrong or misguided about their customer; instead, this decision was made because of the marketing executive's belief that advertising for this product needed to have an "emotional" appeal above all else— a belief that was based on his previous experience as a health-care administrator. We explained that his approach was a consumer one that would resonate with end users, but unless the company was able to "sell" its product to businesses and give the administrators the tools to sell it internally, the opinion of the actual users meant little at this point.

Our advice was ignored. A few months later, the company's ad campaign was rolled out, and the response was a deafening silence. The problem was that the company's advertising never came close to communicating the message it needed to. The ads should have outlined the benefits of the product to businesses, and the marketing strategy should have included a business-focused brochure, testimonials, and features; instead, the material created was vague, image-oriented advertising that looked far more like a Benetton fashion promotion than a service ad for large corporations.

In short, the advertising did not work. Nobody who wasn't already familiar with the company and its product could gauge what the ads were talking about, and the audience the company was shooting for didn't find enough substance in the ads, brochures, and promotional material to justify paying the $30-a-month per employee to have it as a value-added benefit.

Wants and Needs are, in the simplest of terms, understanding the desires and motivations of your client. If you can't nail down whom you're talking to and how you need to speak to them, no amount of pretty images will make up for that misstep.

The Case for B2B Branding

According to The American Marketing Association, **branding** is defined as a:

"Name, term, sign, symbol, or design, or a combination of them intended to identify the goods and services of one seller or group of sellers and to differentiate them from those of other sellers."

Branding is many things. It's your logo. It's your message. It's your company's "attitude." Branding simplifies big ideas, makes complicated descriptions easy to digest and (when necessary) sexy and inviting. Branding defines how you project yourself to the outside world, particularly to your customer. Branding also forces your company to answer the fundamental question of how the world should perceive you and, as a results, embrace you, your products, or your service.

On average, smaller companies tend to look at branding as a waste of energy, time, and money. The direct approach—i.e., selling a particular product to a particular audience within a particular timeframe at a particular posted price—is as complicated as it needs to be. Others believe branding is necessary for large, institutional companies but not for local mom-and-pop businesses. The third reason often cited is that the selling of B2B products inevitably comes down to price.

Although each of these positions has some element of validity, one thing above all is true: you cannot compare the kind of strategy an IBM or Constant Contact will have to pursuing new business with a local financial advisor or auto parts distributor. However, for every business that knows you exist, there are just as many, or more, that are unfamiliar with you or don't think of you immediately when the need for your product or service presents itself. In a global economy where so many companies compete in the same space together, you simply cannot afford to be misunderstood or undefined to your customers.

Furthermore, the pricing issue assumes that B2B buyers are not swayed by reasonable arguments, familiar brand names, or a company's reputation. Yet according to a 2007 B2B Branding Study for Globalization, pricing becomes a consideration only after a shortlist of contenders is chosen. Who gets on the shortlist? Companies whose "brands" are known to the decision makers. Companies should never view branding as a necessary evil. It is the first and best way for your salespeople—i.e., the lifeblood of your company—to have a good starting point for communicating with potential customers.

As an example of branding, I have a company called "Good Soup." We are a marketing agency. For those who are familiar with us, the name is an offshoot of how I explained my company's philosophy to potential clients. Our brand was built around the idea that effective marketing is a custom recipe for every client. The ingredients are always different, depending on each client's needs and the end users the client wants to reach. One "recipe" (i.e., marketing strategy) might include direct mail and online promotions. Another may consist of print advertising and online initiatives. Others might require more PR and social marketing. These individual recipes, as I liked to explain, were like creating soup. Each one has a personality and a flavor unique to the chef. My wife is Japanese, and this philosophy resonates even more in her culture, where

Ramen chefs are held in high regard for their unique recipes.

I saw this metaphor as an easy way to educate clients about my process without getting bogged down in the particulars of how other agencies do business. Different companies will always find different ways to frame their benefits.

Moreover, taking the time to "brand" your B2B company is a particularly good use of energy, given that the reticence of your competitors to do the same will probably not change in the near future. As a result, you are given the unique advantage of creating the kind of compelling and memorable messaging and brand identity that can go far in putting your company upfront in a potential customer's mind, at the expense of your less enlightened competitor.

Consistent branding, and the materials that accompany it, are built for new eyes as well as familiar ones. It is the first and best way to stand out from the crowd – and standing out is the real goal, isn't it?

Embracing "Out-of-the-Box" Marketing Ideas

In the 1947 Christmas classic *Miracle on 34th Street*, Santa Claus is hired to work for Macy's. Early in the movie, his employer chastises him for doing something few companies would ever approve: sending customers to a competitor (in this case, another department store) to purchase products they couldn't find at their own store. Much to the surprise and delight of Macy's top brass, this earnest approach to customer service turns out to be an unexpected financial boon for the store. Infrequent shoppers felt the attention to their needs was admirable and, as a result, Macy's curried favor with them and won permanent customers in the process.

The lesson here is that a unique, risk-taking, out-of-the-box approach to marketing can differentiate forward-thinking companies from those that just go through the motions. There will always be new strategies for selling. Some will work. Some won't. But those that experiment and have the constitution for risk have generally proven to be winners.

While the *Miracle on 34th Street* "technique" has been adopted by social marketing gurus (who tout the benefits of free information and customer service-based strategies against the shill of "old" marketing), many other "new" approaches to getting customers attention have surfaced over the last few decades, and many more have yet to be discovered.

For example, while doing work on Canon Broadcast several years back, the agency I was with, Marcomm Group, proposed the idea of a publication-based newsletter that could be handed out at trade shows. *Profiles in Excellence* was a 10-panel newspaper-sized "magazine" that grouped all the year's case studies into one colorful publication. It proved to be a huge success and has been a mainstay for more than eight years.

Another marketing agency (Gem Group NY) came up with the idea of seeding the education market with materials that help teachers supplement their classroom curricula. For A&E, that meant creating a new teacher's aid / promotional program for every new history or literature-based film that premiered, such as *Les Misérables* and *St. Patrick*. The aid included discussion points as well as creative contests inspired by the subject of the show. The winner would earn money for their school system, while runners-up would receive any number of added-value prizes.

Boise Cascade, a B2B company that sells paper products, created a very memorable and successful promotion many years ago called "Boise High," which significantly increased the company's sales. Given that their target base were 18-to-49-year-old female administrative assistants and office managers, the challenge to find a new and interesting angle for promotion was considerable. Rather than focusing on the competition and using the tools of the past, the company honed in on the psychology of its audience and scored a home run by filtering the company's products benefits through the common touchstone of high school.

Based on the theme of a 1964 yearbook (also the year the company began business), it focused on a romance between the head cheerleader and football captain, fictional characters Judy Morehead and Steve Gerald. The promotional yearbook (and product catalog) mixed office products with class pictures, dances, school sports and other events. The online component included an "update" on Judy and Steve's relationship in addition to Boise products on special. They also created an interactive community page that allowed customers to vote on what they believed the outcome of Steve and Judy's romance would be. To participate you had to become part of their email list.

In Boise's case, thinking outside of the rigid box of B2B marketing was an unqualified plus. Why? Poisoned gas. Something new amidst ideas often old and overused. Bring an element of surprise or innovation to your marketing materials and you just may find your customers taken notice of you when they previously barely knew you existed.

"Think Different" Wasn't Just a Slogan

The gold statuette for out-of-the-box marketing will always reside, in my opinion, with Apple. While many point to their 1984 commercial as one of the boldest moments in advertising history, I believe that Apple's "Think Different" campaign from 1997 was a much more effective and unique marketing approach. Most computers up to that point were promoted to consumers as either coveted alien monoliths that harbored exciting secrets few could imagine, or were boredom personified in copy-heavy ads with bullet points galore.

We also should bear in mind that fifteen years ago, Apple computers were niche-market products. Graphic designers loved them, and schools loved them, but the average Joe and Jane used the Microsoft platforms at work. They knew HP and IBM and Dell. The "marketing speak" of the moment nearly always favored PCs over Apple, and Apple was in no shape to argue with them. Their advertising budgets were not as robust or aggressive as the PC's. Their products were more expensive. Their usability was relatively unknown outside of those who bought their products. When Steve Jobs took over again in the late '90s, all that changed. The introduction of the iMac and the "Think Different" campaign broke through the clutter and made true believers out of many who weren't.

From the start, Steve Jobs didn't feel the need to cultivate a way of expressing his company's philosophy to his audience. That philosophy already existed and was what motivated his every move. He saw Apple as more than just a seller of computer products and software. His personality and goals defined the company. His desire was to do something "different" and not just give that thought lip service.

He also saw that the consumer market for computers was severely lacking in any kind of break-the-clutter advertising. Competitors did the same thing: fancy ads with little more than eye candy to set them apart. His approach was to do the opposite. Spare ads. Simple messaging. An idea rather than a pitch. When the "Think Different" campaign hit, it was an attention grabber. It was spare, whereas other campaigns were busy. It was thoughtful, whereas other campaigns were flat. It showed people rather than product. Even if this campaign were a failure in the computer market, it would embed the name Apple in the mind of consumers and, therefore, succeed in its first goal: to raise awareness. And in the end, the message had the kind of substance the competitors were lacking but never understood why. Know your company. Know your product – and realize that even people who buy for business purposes expect to be persuaded by more than a "$100 off" sticker.

The New Marketing/Media Landscape: History, Benefits And Drawbacks

Not long ago, audiences expected a certain standard in their media. Movies were slick Hollywood productions. Books and magazines had a familiar "professionalism," and industrial films were heavy with interviews and workmanlike animation. Media that came up short in these forms were considered unpalatable and, to a greater degree, untrustworthy. Sure, the random film or song, grass roots magazine, or self-published manifesto still worked its way into popular culture, but those incidents were few and far between.

Today, it's a completely different story. "Slickness" is considered untrustworthy. Corporate advertising is shunned in favor of homegrown "reviews" on YouTube and comment threads in forums. The look of video has also changed. Where our newscasters and filmmakers used to require studio lights, controlled sets, and high-end film or digital stock, we find cell phone cameras taking their place in breaking news reports. Movies like *Paranormal Activity*, produced in the filmmaker's home, using prosumer cameras, have become acceptable to most audience eyes. As this rough-and-tumble appearance has transformed the norm for new media, "truth" in advertising has found new footing in what I'll refer to as the *amateur aesthetic.* Corporate B2B video, along with everything else, has now undergone a transformation thanks to it.

For many, this aesthetic is neither new nor original—and the only thing surprising about it is how long it has taken to gain hold in our culture. The amateur aesthetic can be traced all the way back to the release of two independent films: 1959's *Shadows* by John Cassavetes and the French film *Breathless* by Jean-Luc Godard the following year.

For those of you unfamiliar with these films, *Shadows* was a quirky, cinema verité improvisation about a group of "beats" (shot at the height of the Beat Generation's cultural pinnacle), one of whom meets and dates a biracial woman. *Breathless*, on the other hand, was a loosely constructed production about a thief who kills a policeman and finds a girl who helps him hide in Italy.

Shadows paved the way for DIY cinema. It is more closely related to contemporary reality-based shows and Robert Altman films than to the dramas that were being made at the time, such as *Anatomy Of A Murder* or *Suddenly, Last Summer*. *Breathless*, a more artistic film and a touchstone of the French New Wave, looked like nothing before it. It was shot hand held with jump cuts, repetitive shots, sloppy edits, and a looseness that resembled home movies. It was hugely influential and emulated in films such as *The Graduate*, *Easy Rider*, and *Slaughterhouse Five*, among others. *Breathless* ushered in this acceptable amateur style that decades later would define music videos, commercials, documentaries, and reality offerings on network and cable television. Unlike the shocked response these groundbreaking films received from the audiences of the 1960s, shaky camera shots, fuzzy images, shoddy audio, and script-free rambles have become commonplace today. As a result, movies, documentaries, and all forms of programming can be produced more cheaply than in the past, and the guidelines for what is considered palatable to a modern audience had more to do with subject matter than production value.

In the last decade, as the Internet morphed from an educational institution resource into a cultural phenomenon, as cable stations offered up hundreds of new programs, and as high-definition hand held cameras became affordable for the masses, the amateur aesthetic grew in acceptability as its media-hungry audience demanded more viewing choices. At first, this was an exciting development. A generation that grew up with three to six channels now had more sources of entertainment than it could fathom. Advertisers merely had to pick and choose from a variety of marketing avenues and tailor their message to specific rather than general audiences. The gates had opened, and exposure was accessible for more than just the biggest companies.

But over time, and as expected, audiences became overwhelmed with too many choices and began to selectively shut out anything not on their priority list. Breaking through the clutter of mass media became much more difficult than it was earlier, even though the entry fee was smaller. Although you can still capture a customer's attention by performing some outrageous promotional stunt that gets media coverage or driving customers to your website through giveaways, these strategies have become predictable for audiences of 20 to 50-year-olds who've seen it all.

In what are now the early 2010s, audiences are more intrigued by the ordinary than the extraordinary. Hand-held customer testimonials on YouTube, awkwardly written recommendations on forums, and one-on-one live podcasts between manufacturers and customers have just as much sway today as the slickest Super Bowl commercial had decades ago. There is a hunger for uncut reality in our entertainment and advertising. When it strikes a chord, the results can be massive.

A good example of this in the consumer space is Rebecca Black's 2011 video *Friday*. This 13-year-old's parents spent a couple of thousand dollars to produce a song and accompanying video that years before would have been cost-prohibitive, and Rebecca became an Internet sensation and a recording industry sensation nearly overnight. At the time I'm writing this, her video on YouTube has had well over 167 million views, and her audio version on iTunes hit number 69 on its first day.

There has been much discussion of the public's reaction to this video, which many consider unworthy of such attention, but in my opinion, it does nearly everything right for today's audience. The song is catchy, the singer is real, and the lyrics and video are off-center enough to make it a unique experience. It breaks the clutter even in a media space where *everyone* is trying to break the clutter. It also succeeds because we, the audience, see the "ordinary" in this girl. She's not a pre-packaged product. She's one of us. It's the same reason American Idol is so popular. We understand her somewhat misdirected approach to starting a music career. We find her lack of professionalism appealing. In short, we root for her. She is the awkward 13-year-old all of us used to be. We quietly cheer her enthusiasm and know that putting yourself out there, considering the risk of humiliation, is worth attention—and we like our products unique, not perfect. It's a lesson not lost on businesses that see their competition taking risks in new media and watching as some actually pay off.

Once again, in a world of *wants* and *needs*, marketers must do more than create a presence for themselves, even one that includes sharp branding. They need to view their audience as a huge crowd on a busy, noisy street. The only way to get anyone's attention under those circumstances is to be either genuine or clever, shout as loud as you can, and always have something interesting and hopefully entertaining and enlightening to say.

Advertising as "Poison Gas"

One of my early bosses, George Lois, has a reputation four decades long for sharp rhetoric and bold creative thinking. Back in the early '70s, he appeared on a talk show hosted by David Susskind, along with several other distinguished members of the advertising industry. When asked by Susskind to define advertising, most of these distinguished gentlemen from large shops waxed philosophical about the history of the business, what the steps were in marketing a product, and, in short, made every attempt to categorize their profession as being no different from any other.

Susskind noticed George's grimaces of disagreement and asked,

"Why are you making those faces, George? Don't you agree with these gentlemen?"

George leaned forward and offered an alternative answer that would define advertising for many generations.

"No. I don't agree," he said. *"Advertising is poison gas. It should bring tears to your eyes. It should unhinge your nervous system. It should knock you out."*

While he was quick to admit that his answer was a bit over the top (and said as a way to differentiate him from the stodgy group he was seated with), his statement couldn't be truer in terms of how smart companies need to approach their marketing challenges. At the end of the day, the loudest and most unique voice is the one that's heard by the largest audience, and it's not always very difficult to be that voice.

Most advertising is invisible, certainly not because it wants to be but because most marketers who create it do not understand its purpose or the varied clients who approve it don't understand its limited potential. As a result, trade channels are filled with ads and campaigns that look vaguely like one another, rarely distinguishing themselves, and become part of the noise rather than offering a clear, concise message. Why is this? Well, the simplest answer is that most agencies do the best they can to create advertising that replicates the look and attitude of other campaigns they deem successful—and, more than anything else, try to please a client who they know has a limited tolerance for ideas too far out of the box. This is not to say the reasoning for these campaigns that exist isn't sound. It's just not exceptional. Exceptional, as in most areas of industry, comes from those who decide *not* to follow the same path everyone else chooses. In the advertising industry, most of the surprising work these days comes from the brains of those who are unabashedly off-center and different. When they do good work in this industry, it is sometimes great. Unfortunately, there are also a lot of advertising people and client-side marketers out there (as there are in most industries) who never give up trying to fit in, and it always shows in the final work produced.

In order for a company to define itself as a brand, it requires that company to call attention to its uniqueness rather than its similarities with competitors. Defining oneself requires a fearless act, not a reticent one, even in the B2B space. Now, that doesn't necessarily mean you launch a marketing stunt that entails Carrot Top running onto the Fenway Park diamond and performing an interpretive dance in your company's T-shirt, but it sure as hell is better than spending thousands, or millions, on a campaign that few remember and even fewer notice.

Good Marketing is About Good Communication

As a child, I assumed that becoming an adult meant I would be able to communicate eloquently, use large words that everyone understood, and be able to elaborate on big concepts in complex ways. Maybe I was the only 10-year-old who thought like that, or quite possibly it was the world at large that took me by surprise when I found out communication for the masses doesn't really work that way.

Good marketing is about good communication and, as most people learn once they become adults (or earlier), good communication is the ability to convey complicated matters through simple words. The masses don't process information the way rocket scientists do. We don't disseminate information through multi-tiered, layered text or speech. Like you and me, most people prefer their conversation, their media, and their advertising in easy-to-understand bits. This is the reason that most consumer advertising, once you strip it down, is simple, clear, and connectable. B2B advertising needs to be the same but rarely is. A typical B2B ad, whether digital or print, is a mass of bullet points and "information" rather than a clear message. There are those who argue that a "quasi-consumer"— or simpler approach—just doesn't work for B2B, but many successful companies have proven that theory false. Certainly you need to know and understand your client. You need to use several marketing channels to push your product or service, and most of those channels will require some customization. But simple, bold ideas will always win out over bland or complex advertising.

Let's look at FedEx. This company, which has always bridged the gap between consumer and B2B, discovered that simple, easy-to-understand big idea years ago, and it catapulted them from an also-ran into one of the most successful companies of the last 50 years. What was that big, yet simple idea? Speed.

The marketing of most of the other mail-carrier companies also focused on speed in one way or another in the past. What they were never able to do, however, is find an effective way to brand it and capture the public zeitgeist. FedEx did do that, and did it beautifully, so much so that its campaign—with its memorable commercials and billion-dollar marketing budget—would have succeeded on a modest budget just as well.

It wasn't always this way for the company. The first FedEx commercial campaigns concentrated on the process of how packages got to where they were going rather than how quickly. Their message was that this new company had its own airline and, therefore, didn't get bogged down with the time-consuming task of moving packages from one commercial flight to another. They were humorous spots, it was a good idea, and one that also targeted a strength, but what was missing was that crucial element that could cultivate an emotional response from a potential customer.

Two years later, in 1981, FedEx introduced what we know today as its signature spot with actor John Moschitta, the fast talker. What's great about this campaign was not only how FedEx found simplicity in its big idea, but how it tied right into its customers' needs: FedEx customers expected everything to be delivered fast and efficiently. They didn't care whether FedEx had its own air transportation. They didn't want to hear about how their packages wouldn't be bumped because someone on that flight had an extra piece of luggage. They assumed any good messenger company would have these efforts under control. Their real concern was whether the company they used actually valued speed, service, and exactitude or if its employees were simply a bunch of pencil pushers who clock in every day, put in their time, and shift through your packages with little more than mechanical obliviousness (as most people thought the Post Office did). The explanation had to resonate with the direct customer as well as their company's "committee" of decision makers.

For the customer, it's never been about the process; it's always been about the results. FedEx's humorous commercials positioned it as a company in fast-motion 24 hours a day, run by people who never bat an eye at the pace of their business because they appear organically built for it.

It was a unique communication. It was bold in a space that was not known for it, and it was remarkably simple. All the earmarks of what great advertising should be.

CHAPTER 2:

Myths Dismantled

Every company exists in a little bit of a bubble—that space where we let our confidence lead and our sense of logic and proportion wane. Sometimes it's egged on by a motivational speech by our superiors or others in the company that frames their strengths and how a little bit of marketing will go a long way in reinforcing what they believe to be an absolute truth; that the benefits of their product or service are so great that customers will literally jump at buying it when they hear about it. Actual marketing results are where the rubber hits the road in this equation, but the surprise companies sometimes have when their baby doesn't take off as expected could be more measured if only a few myths about marketing were revealed and reinforced. While this list is hardly complete it's handy to know. Only when we face the truth can we invest in the tools and strategies that'll help us overcome our business obstacles and really make the most of our marketing dollars.

Myth #1: Customers Know a Lot About Your Product or Service Already

Meeting with new clients has always been a pleasure for me. Not only because I enjoy meeting new people and welcome the challenge of new projects, but also because I'm naturally curious as to how companies view themselves from the inside. Sometimes my job has been easy, particularly when a client company has a real world view of who it is, what its marketing challenges are, and smart strategies for overcoming them.

Many times, however, I find companies that display an impressive expertise at their business and are well-versed in the details of what they have to offer, but they have little to no idea of what their customers are really, truly looking for or thinking. Most of these meetings focus less on the overall strategies for marketing and more on discussion of an innovative product element, a laundry list of items that *must* be used as bullet points, and a partial blindness to selling features or untouched market segments that are right under their noses.

Whether you're an established business or not, if you're not advertising to a particular strength, feature, or brand identity, you could find yourself an also-ran in categories where you deserve to be front-runner.

For all the testing, experimentation, and false starts that can make up a campaign, there is still a science to marketing. As well, there are expectations from every audience (often dictated by previous marketing efforts that have succeeded). It's also wise to learn from your competitors. You should never ignore the success of someone else within your market because it's inconvenient for your own efforts.

Lets look at UPS now. UPS's early advertising, like FedEx's, was unremarkable and focused on saying similar things about speed and accuracy but without the off-the-wall humor. Eventually, UPS found its voice and its own unique character. The UPS Whiteboard commercials assumed the audience knew that their packages would get there on time. What UPS adopted as its own unique selling proposition was its ability to predict all the logistical nightmares customers might have and to offer their clients built-in solutions that addressed them. According to Andy Azula, Creative Director for The Martin Agency and the face of the Whiteboard commercials themselves, their goal was to refresh their successful *"What Can Brown Do For You"* campaign by discussing all the parts and pieces of UPS products and services and, as a result, reach all their business audiences at once.

The Whiteboard commercials are simple and informative in the same way Dyson vacuum commercials are. They don't try to "sell" their audience through pure entertainment or visual flair but, instead, talk to them as educated customers. In the new world of personalized marketing, where companies try hard to connect as well as inform new prospects, UPS's matter-of-fact, conversational approach fits right in to the current groove.

UPS never assumed that the public understood its history, service, and safeguards. It took the view that most of the public was still unfamiliar with most of what they had to offer. It was this ability to stand outside of its company culture and take the point-of-view of the customer that aided UPS's successful efforts.

Unless you are a known brand, you must assume that your new customer is completely ignorant of what you have to offer them, even if you've been a player in your category for a long time. As an example, Canon was known industry-wide for its exceptional lenses and lens technologies. What most people weren't aware of was that Canon has also been a player in the network security space for a very long time. Its product line, known as Network Video Solutions, not only rivaled its competitors but also surpassed them in terms of connectivity and built-in software features. Until recently, most of the customers for these products were familiar with Axis as the key security manufacturer, thanks to Axis' consistent advertising in trade magazines, its robust online presence, and its vast dealer network.

But once Canon began advertising in force in the last few years, the audience became aware that there was now another formidable player in this market. Canon could have rested on its laurels and assumed that as the number one brand in the lens market, it was automatically recognized in the security market as well. Had it not been for its ability to think outside of its corporate culture in the way FedEx and UPS did, Canon executives could be scratching their heads over why customers weren't responding as planned. Instead, they are working hard to keep up with demand for products that, thanks to effective marketing, have finally stood out from the crowd.

Myth #2: Customers Don't Want to Be "Sold" to

Do you get a lot of calls from solicitors and marketing companies during dinner? I sure do. Whether it's a local fundraising organization or a phone company hawking a new service, the intrusion is, and will always be, unwelcome. I do my best to be courteous, but it's often difficult. The calls are an interruption of my family time and an uninvited one at that. It should come as no surprise, however, that the companies at the other end of the line feel the exact opposite of how I do. For them, it's a numbers game. If they call 20 people and one or two sign up for their service or make a contribution, their strategy is a success.

Could this be categorized as bad advertising? Maybe, if I were their only potential customer, but given that these companies DO get sales through this approach, they're obviously doing something right.

There are many new books out there about how social marketing has changed the conversation. One of its well-held covenants is that the kind of marketing described above is no longer the way people care to be sold to. Dozens of these books have been published in the last few years that attempt to convince us indirectly that human beings have actually changed in the past few generations. They suggest that Generation X cannot be swayed with ads that have too many exclamation points in them—and that billboards, TV commercials, and print ads are no longer an effective means of communication, or at the very least not the preferred means. The new meme is that advanced human beings of today prefer to choose how and when they communicate with marketing and don't want to be bothered with anything that isn't what we refer to as a "soft sell." Today's customers, according to this theory, are only viable customers after they've read an article you've published and let it sink in for some future sale or responded to a call-to-action form of their own volition when they really, truly were interested. Otherwise, your conventional marketing methods will fail you, or worse, turn your potential customers off so completely they will curse your brand name should they ever hear it again.

This is what some would like you to believe, but if this line of thought were actually true, then how do we account for the huge number of cold-call phone sales that are successful? How do we account for the massive amount of companies that *do* make money without having a robust online strategy? How do you account for the fact that every major manufacturer *still* advertises in trade magazines, on TV, and through tried-and-true public relations channels, even when some of these channels are considered passé?

Here's the simple truth. Marketing can't *always* be about the "soft sell." It can't always be about waiting for that customer to come to you or counting the visitors who've found you on the web. That is why the conventional methods of marketing (ads, TV or web campaigns, articles in prominent trade magazines) still work. When a salesperson becomes tangible—a voice at the end of the phone or someone on TV or in a video banner ad telling you what you should want—the potential for making the sale or simply embedding your message in the mind of the potential buyer is considerable. All new methods of marketing are useful and effective, mind you. I engage in them and use them every single day I work. But when my agency puts together a strategy for a marketing campaign, all options are on the table and, more often than not, we'll draw from both sides of the media trough.

We already know not every company is braced to benefit from new media. Not in 2012. Possibly not in 2013. Some never. My brother, for example, runs a company that sells computer supplies over the phone. His sales people focus primarily on referrals, leads and cold calls. They've tried online marketing: built an e-commerce site, did their due diligence with regard to getting it placed, did keyword advertising, the whole shebang. But the site didn't make even a fraction of what their sales people did, despite the considerable investment of time and money. Are they right and are the gurus wrong? No. My brother's clients, like many in B2B professions, didn't want to simply buy their supplies from a website and hope for the best, despite the good testimonials they'd find there. They make purchases in bulk. The money used to make these purchases isn't pocket change. The reputation of these employees is on the line with every decision they make, particularly these days and in this economy. Therefore, for Reliant Computer Supplies and its clients, a phone conversation with a real salesperson is mandatory. Questions need to be asked. Someone needs to be responsible.

Am I saying that the gurus are 100% wrong about how new media is changing the sales landscape? Absolutely not. For B2C, it's obviously working. Both forms of marketing are effective, but neither can be self-sufficient for every client, and you, the reader, may be that exception. For a buyer in a large B2B company, your ability to break through the clutter, as always, will make a difference, but the "soft sell" promoted in today's business books will not close the deal alone. Only sales people can do that, and the first step is to accept that people *do* want to be sold to.

Back to my dinnertime phone calls: Let's focus on the one or two who *do* respond to this heavy-handed approach. These people, more times than not, are predisposed to the sale before the call has even been made. I encountered these folks when I did phone sales for Publishers Clearing House as a young man. And my sales pitch sucked. Nonetheless, I was able, through sheer numbers, to find these people and make the sale. Even if you were as bad a phone salesman as I was, those customers actually *want* you to succeed in selling them and might reward you with the sale if you make your case. In business exchanges, these are those same folks who see opportunity in your product or service. They want to find something that will better their lives and that of their company. It is the opposite of an impulse buy. So don't believe anyone who tells you the "tried-and-true methods" are no longer valid. It's just not true—not until the writing is etched into the stone.

Conventional marketing still works for a vast majority of people in the B2B space. It does well for modest sales, but it also does so particularly well for high-priced items. The fact is, we expect quality products companies to spend money promoting themselves. If these products are worth their weight, they are surely worth the time, energy, and cost of making a name for themselves in the public forum and not just push a blog post through their LinkedIn feed as the beginning and end of their marketing initiative.

Myth #3: Our Previously Successful Advertising Campaign Doesn't Need to Be Updated

Throughout the '80s, '90s, and early 2000s, Microsoft was at the top of its game. Its stock soared, its market share was enormous, and its brand was infallible. Today, the company is scrambling.

Make no mistake. Microsoft is far from a struggling company, but it has been struggling for some time to secure its top name recognition in a category where it has been the market leader for decades. Its failure to maintain this spot seems to have had as much to do with inertia and culture (Microsoft has always been a follower as a company, whereas Apple has defined itself as an innovator), as it had to do with its marketing.

Where Apple's advertising has always been fresh, Microsoft's often felt derivative. Its "I'm a PC" campaign owes a lot to Apple's "What's in Your PowerBook?" campaign from 2003, as well as the "Mac" and "PC" ads starring actor Justin Long. Microsoft's products have been slow to the market, and its brand has not taken advantage of brick and mortar in the way Apple has. As a result, Microsoft is no longer the name on the tip of everyone's tongue when they think of who's the biggest icon in the personal computer industry.

Marketing campaigns, no matter how effective, will always require a "reboot" at one point or another. What worked yesterday may have been great, but audiences are always changing (getting older as well as getting younger), and messages that don't grow and adapt get stale. For example, large companies don't revamp their campaigns every few years because their marketing managers are bored. They do it to infuse some new life into their products, services, and brand name. Some capitalize on their past, but only if it positions them as a category mainstay or helps them to be seen as the company of the future.

For example, Mercedes uses its history in its marketing campaign to reinforce the steadiness and quality of its product. The company wants to frame innovation as a process and not a single act. Other companies rework their brand to let customers know they are moving forward. Computer Associates shunned the past by changing its name in 2006 to CA Technologies. It was an effective way to link CA's expanding line of services as well as connect with a digital world that sees "computers" as a fading vessel for a much larger industry. Canon, as well, altered its long-held tagline, "Canon Know How," to the more digitally oriented "ImageAnyware." The new tagline talks to universal quality of the Canon brand as well as the inter-connectivity of its products—and images that can be viewed, printed, and transferred anywhere to any connected Canon product. As a result, they are always fresh even when the company's technological history is its real story.

Marketing reboots are also not the exclusive domain of large, multinational corporations. Smaller businesses, particularly busy ones, are always the last to recognize that their materials have dated them. At the end of the day, companies large and small need to institutionalize the idea of doing a refresh. The business world at large moves way too fast for any company brand to be seen as stale.

Myth #4: The Internet Has Changed Everything

Are you selling products or services to consumers? Are you a marketing company with a desire to have potential clients learn your philosophy? Are you an established B2C company looking for a new way to connect with your customers? If so, the Internet *has* changed everything for you. But if you're a company that sells pool pallets to large importers, well, a presence on the web and a social marketing strategy may not be the savior it is to others.

Let's face it. There is little way in which a blog by a pool pallet company is going to electrify the 45-year-old supply manager who needs to purchase 75 pallets for several ports. Now, a pool pallet company can come up with some truly interesting content for the web. Maybe an article that really shines a light on how pallets are used, how shipping has changed, how the company's product or service is unique from the rest. Maybe this company is even finding remarkable ways to connect the creation of the pool pallet to some deep life philosophy. Who knows? What's true, however, is that most companies like this pool pallet outfit won't benefit from online social interactions and direct-to-consumer offers the way other companies will.

Let's take a look at a company that has benefitted hugely from social media. IBM is one of those companies that has developed a culture that's social marketing friendly. A huge number of IBM employees blog or tweet, and that's encouraged by Big Blue. As a result, IBM has developed a wide range of followers for its products and services through the popularity of these employees, and they utilize these connections.

For its Global Conference, Impact, IBM unleashed a Twitter campaign that promised to those who sign up within the first 72 hours a chance to talk for 30 minutes with Jerry Cuomo, Vice- President and COO of its popular business integration software, WebSphere (more on that in Chapter 10, *Success Stories*).

The more pertinent question is whether a firm like that pool pallet company *can* find customers through new media channels? The answer is yes. Of course they can. So can anyone. They can go on PalletForum.com and offer good advice to those with questions. They can produce PR that secures a prime spot in American Shipper, both on and offline, and send out customized emails through AmericanShipper.com's opt-in list. They can put banner advertisements on that site. They can go to the Food Service Conference through PMA, set up a booth, advertise in the trade show journal, deliver a fresh-fruit container on a miniature pool pallet to all potential client rooms at the convention's connected hotel, with a reminder to visit the company's booth while in town. They can have an interactive pool pallet durability test game set up on an LCD screen at the booth to reinforce why this company's pallets are the hardiest on the market. There are options.

Unfortunately, the company probably won't benefit from creating a Facebook "Like" page, or from developing a promotion to win a trip to America's most beautiful ports, or from trying to get customers to comment on its blog post "10 Ways Pool Pallets Reduce Shipping Costs." Those 45-year-old supply managers are too busy filling out forms and purchase orders in their proprietary software and, if they are browsing the Internet, it is probably for personal interests like most of the country (and world). And all of this comes down to your customer's profile.

My goal as a marketing expert has always been about being

honest with my clients. Selling them a service because it's hot (and, therefore, may be easier to sell) isn't doing them any favors and reduces my value as a useful resource. Marketing managers at companies need to be equally pragmatic about what they truly need and how their marketing dollars are spent. Anyone can suggest a new website or a Twitter account, but is it really what you need and, if you do need it, are you willing to put in the time and effort—and have the patience—to see it through?

Myth #5: Blogging Automatically Leads to New Customers

Whether it's a consumer, B2B, or niche model, blogging is hard. It is time consuming. It does not always pay dividends in the short term, no matter how hard you work at it, unless you hit it big with an article or post that taps into the public zeitgeist—and THAT is what most blogging books won't tell you is the key, and the hardest thing to do. Imagine if someone told you that you could become an expert at filmmaking and all you had to do was produce a hit film. Easier said than done. Blogging is the number one suggestion in all the social marketing books, and I'm here to tell you it's not a quick fix for anything or a guaranteed path to marketing success, unless you're a celebrity or celebrity blogger. Useful? Yes. Productive? Certainly. Potentially beneficial financially? As with anything we put our mind to, you bet. And with business-to-business, it's decidedly true that you need only a few good leads for your blog strategy to be a success. But understand this above everything else: it's about putting the time in and not expecting a return right away. When it comes to business blogging, you need to take the following to heart:

1. **Blogging is branding:**

Although your opinion is as important as your personality, the subtext of your blog posts should be a continuation of brand awareness. Your audience is looking for information from someone in the know, but your goal should always be to direct it back to your brand.

2. **It's always about the content:**

Ann Handley & C.C. Chapman, the authors of *Content Rules*, put it very simply and elegantly: *"Produce great stuff, and your customers will come to you. Produce really great stuff, and your customers will share and disseminate your message for you."* Content is king on the web, and the sole purpose of your blog is to "speak" to and educate your potential customers. By becoming the voice they seek for advice in your particular business category, strangers can become clients, and clients can help get you more clients.

3. **Don't shill:**

The last thing anyone has time to listen to these days is a boring pitch. The only people still open to this kind of approach were my grandparents, who grew up during the early days of marketing and didn't know anything different. Audiences today are savvy and have seen and heard it all. As I mentioned earlier, honesty and genuineness in your posts will go a long way in getting your potential customers to trust you. Who would you rather spend time listening to: a slick used-car salesman or the smart guy next door? No brainer, this one.

4. **Don't stop:**

The number one reason blogs fail for business is because they never had the chance to succeed in the first place. Building an audience takes patience, and if you're planning to call it quits after one or two posts, you don't really want to pursue this. It takes a sacrifice of time on your part and a commitment.

Now, if you're willing to make the sacrifice, willing to do the work, and committed to the idea that your blog is as much a reflection of who you are as it is a marketing tool for what you do, you will in the end succeed at making it such.

One of the better success stories that reflects this type of hard work is Brandtelling.com. Started by Arthur Germain, a brand marketing strategist who began his company Communication Strategy Group in 2005, Brandtelling.com sticks closely to Seth Godin's theory that blogging is not purely about creating revenue. It's about your ability to write and communicate well, to develop consistent, shareable content rather than eye candy and, by virtue of becoming better at it, advancing your mission and view of the world in a very concise way.

Arthur created his blog back in 2006. He was one of the first marketing people to catch the Twitter wave and integrate it into his daily (or weekly) conversations. He also used his blog as a connecting thread to all other social outlets—Facebook, LinkedIn, YouTube, and an RSS feed—and built those as well. His LinkedIn profile is a perfect example of how to focus your efforts and network (more about all this later). His articles are what blogging is all about: providing useful information for his clients and his potential clients at no charge, and projecting his expertise in the process.

Although none of his articles has gone viral in a way that would make him an automatic Thought Leader for the masses, he has become one nonetheless, because blogging is about micro-conversations, and those types of conversations are no different from meeting a prospective client at a trade show and

talking him or her up. In the end, if it results in more business, it's a successful strategy. Arthur's micro-conversations
have done that. To date, his Twitter account is 1,107 followers
strong; his LinkedIn profile is always active with feeds and has
over 500 connections; and his Facebook account is a robust
mix of business and personal, as it should be.

Has all of this work, in the end, paid off for Arthur with
new business? Yes it has, but let me add a wrinkle. It paid off
for him through the integration of his offline efforts as well.
Arthur has spent a lot of time speaking in public and at
industry events. He frequents trade shows and, at times, has
had booths of his own. He gets his name out there any way
he can that fits his strategy, similar to how he helps his own
clients succeed. He is not just throwing the ball; he is the
ball. Any good marketing or public relations strategy requires
offline and online measures today. The theory that *everything*
is doable through the web is farce. You can't become a movie
director by sitting home and watching movies all day. At some
point, you have to pull yourself up from the couch, brush away
the Cheetos, and make it happen.

Taking the above advice for what it is, a blog is only useful
to a B2B company if that company has the time to post, the
interest in posting, the stamina to keep doing it, and a desire to
write that isn't motivated by profit. As is the case with Arthur,
you can become a thought leader, depending on how saturated
your category is, but it will take as much time and effort as it
has getting you into the position you have in your company.
Nothing in blogging is fast and easy.

Although I still recommend you create new content, there
are ways other than blogging to find your audience, engage
them, and get leads doing so. More on that later.

Myth #6: "New" Marketing Doesn't Need "Traditional" to Succeed

As I mentioned in the last chapter, there is a view out there that social marketing can be a cure-all for companies that may not have the budget for big advertising and PR. For some of those companies, social marketing can and will provide a cost-effective outlet that didn't exist before. It's not a stretch to believe that a custom-pan-rack designer who has trouble getting his product sold through the most well-known distributors for restaurants and food service outlets around the country might have better luck selling through RestaurantEquipment-World.com and getting a mention on its blog. That same company can also benefit from a market-specific website as well (see Chapter 6). But more times than not, when the old methods of advertising and PR are applied smartly and in conjunction with "new," they will further a company's reach much more effectively than 30 blog posts on its own website will.

While consumers search for the advice and reviews of products from like-minded counterparts, business people are more wary of a critique on a forum as any kind of definitive research on their next purchase. And the higher-priced the item is, the more convincing they will need—and *need*, once again, is the defining term when talking about this audience.

In many markets, advertising in conventional trade channels is more than just an afterthought. It can define whether a company is considered a player. Furthermore, an article on a product or service in respected trade media, particularly by a reviewer with a reputation, will cancel out the amateur opinions of countless bloggers. And that is the way it has always been, even today. A positive article on a company or product in The Wall Street Journal can set that company on jet propulsion. A product that makes it to HSN can, alone, catapult an unknown inventor into the stratosphere. Although these channels can be difficult to reach for the marketer with a limited budget, it can be accomplished.

And as far as those amateur bloggers are concerned, even some of them become superstars in their own right. Engadget.com started out as amateur blogs created by Peter Rojas. Today, Engadget is ranked 5th in the Technorati top 1001 and is the go-to site if you want your new electronics product well known. There is a value in the reputation of Engadget, and savvy electronics customers know this. Banner ads for your product have a unique advantage on sites like these as well.

The same goes for Reviewed.com. Ever heard of it? Unless you are in the consumer or professional camera or camcorder business, probably not. Still, the site is an absolute must in terms of camera and camcorder reviews. CEO Robin Liss began this venture as a 13-year-old electronics buff who enjoyed trying camera equipment and posting reviews on her personal blog. By the time she enrolled at Tufts University, she had an operation that consisted of 12 employees and a cadre of sites, including CamcorderInfo.com, DigitalCameraInfo.com, and others. Her reviews were thorough and included camera testing as well, not just personal opinion. As such, she became a Thought Leader in this category. Companies including Canon, Panasonic, Sony, and others would send free products to her to review, and her income came from an enormous amount of banner advertising on these sites. In short, she created her own publishing empire by the time she was in her early 20s.

There are many successful stories like Liss and Rojas in several B2B spaces. And, if you're lucky, there may be a lack of Thought Leaders in your own business space, which provides you with the perfect opportunity to fill that niche.

Consumer marketers? Sure, they can probably go it alone

and, with a good amount of ingenuity and social smarts, make a name for themselves and their product or service simply because the audience numbers are on their side and the blogosphere embraces consumer-friendly media more easily. But B2B doesn't have that flexibility, and until things change forever in that space, you still need to consider combining your new strategies with a few of the old ones that still work.

Myth #7: Marketing Agencies Aren't Needed. We Can Do It All In-House

Big, multi-national corporations understand the need for marketing. Even though the arguments about ROI are ever-present, most will agree that staying in front of customers, touting new innovations, and always selling—whether it's in person or from an advertisement—is a valid use of time.

Some smaller companies, particularly those new to marketing themselves, will tend to question the immediate effectiveness of these initiatives and also mistakenly assume they can get a lot for very little. As such, they may start by creating their marketing in-house. They hire a graphic designer; get some computer software and a desk. They start up their Facebook, Twitter, and LinkedIn accounts. They might even hire a company to produce a video. In short order, however, they discover that the graphic designer doesn't know how to concept, the office manager doesn't have any idea how to place ads or what those crazy formats they're given means, and their elements don't seem to work together, all of it simply becoming a crazy quilt of mismatched messages, unproductive social marketing attempts, and materials that require reprints due to low-resolution images and lack of page bleed.

At the end of this familiar fiasco, they finally resolve to hire an agency. Although that's a positive step, many still believe their lofty goals can be accomplished for the same price of an intern and a junior designer.

Our agency generally functions on monthly retainers; however, we do project work as well. Creative and strategy is covered under the retainer. Production is separate. Public Relations tends to have a budget all its own (because the skills needed are unique to that practice). This structure is built so that the client gets use of us in the most efficient way possible, has senior people attached to the client's account (and most of the time attached as that client's only account) and a team that is thinking of new ways to service this client even when we're between projects. We've always understood our job is to think through every possible scenario, look at every angle, and come up with new and unique methods of taking our clients' products and services and placing them in front of the audience they desire. To do that, we need experienced people. Experienced people do not grow on trees, even in a down economy. Those people have to know how to work together and be efficient. They have to know the ins and outs of their client's category. They have to be on top of every new innovation in their field and their client's. They have to have relationships with publications and trade show events. They need to be able to negotiate aggressively with printers and programmers and know whether the latest social marketing "must" is truly worthwhile or another rip-off.

This entire team of people must, in essence, function as the best full-time marketing employee this client ever had. So the real question for a client or company, after they've ascertained that they need marketing help, is how much it would cost to hire all those people in-house to accomplish the goals they've set for themselves.

And how much, exactly, would that cost in real-world terms. Monthly retainers vary from agency to agency. Assume that the monthly retainer for The Martin Agency from Volkswagen is enormous. Yours probably isn't. But it's easier to find an agency that fits your size than it is to pick a small price and try to find someone to produce for it. You will inevitably get that person, or persons. But how much will it cost you before you find yourself once again looking at real agency work and wondering why your own suffers by comparison?

Myth #8: ROI Happens Right Away

I had a client some time back that asked my agency to develop an ad for him. We did. We also offered him a media plan for getting eyes on the ad and other measures we could take to further its reach. He looked at the plan and said, "No. I just want to run the ad once in one magazine. If it doesn't do what we need it to do with that one placement, it won't do it at all." Sure enough, we ran the ad in the one magazine and, while the response was reasonable, it was not the "landslide" the client was expecting. As a result, that client never ran another ad.

Now, did this client receive enough of a return on investment for his outlay with us? Hard to tell—because marketing is rarely a one-off. Branding and message recognition is about consistency and repetition, and although I would never fault a company for watching its bottom line, not every service in the world is as cut and dry as, say, the electric company. A marketing plan, whether new media or old, is a process. Sometimes the benefits of that process are immediate, but more often than not, they take time. That is why media and marketing plans are developed a year at time. You set your goals and methodically move to reach them. As long as you are doing what you can to engage your audience, are open to new ideas, and don't shortchange yourself, benefits will be seen so the next time your salespeople ask potential clients if they've heard of you, they'll say yes. Then you'll know that several months as the lead banner of the most popular trade website and a clever campaign touting your product's benefits have risen to the surface. If you do very little in the way of marketing, you can be sure your customers' response will be no.

Myth #9: It's All About Style

Before acknowledging anything else, the first conclusion you need to make is that your product or services IS unique. It's unique in the same way YOU are unique. Unless you are creating wholesale replicas of other products and services out there, note for note, and promoting it—note for note— exactly the same way as the competition, you should have at least one unique selling feature to offer your audience. Although it's true that sometimes B2B business is predicated on budget and reputation, that doesn't mean the world is suddenly equal in the eyes of the buyer. Sure. Features are important. If you want to clutter your ad with nothing but bullet points, that is your prerogative. If you feel a fancy series of typefaces, color bars, and drop shadows will help you stand out from the crowd in a busy periodical, go for it. But it is not the best use of your time when developing your marketing materials, nor is it the takeaway you want from your audience.

The most important part of your marketing plan is your message. Apple knows this. FedEx knows this—and thousands upon thousands of other successful companies realize this as well. It is what you say, how you say it, and how you visualize it that will, in the end, make a difference and truly resonate for the buyer. You can have those bullets points in there as well, but without a cohesive, clear, and attractive message, you won't pull away from the pack. Why are there so few marketing campaigns we can point to as unique and memorable? Well, inspired creativity that matches needs and expectations isn't as common as most would hope. But the first step to achieving that kind of marketing success resides in your approach. Know your company. Know your product—and realize that even people who buy for business purposes expect to be persuaded by more than a "$100-off" sticker.

CHAPTER 3:

The Advantage Most B2B Businesses Don't Know They Have

Take a good, hard look at banner ads or print in any trade website or magazine. Notice anything familiar? Most of the marketing you'll find there is completely and utterly forgettable. More than that, it's not even trying to be memorable. Now, notice the one or two ads that did manage to catch your attention? See a similarity between them? Chances are, they have a unique voice, a quick-to-read image that explains the service without words, and a clean, clutter-free look. You've just noticed the difference between effective ads and the other 99%.

A significant deal of advertising in the B2B space is unremarkable. It's boring. It is all about fitting as much information, offers, and unnecessary graphics on a page as it can hold. And it doesn't do the job it's supposed to.

Now, grab a Rolling Stone, a Wired or a Forbes. Although there will also be forgettable ads in these magazines, there will probably be a few more that work. Ads in these publications, and their accompanying websites, are much more expensive to place. The weight of an ad's effectiveness is as important as the page it sits on. In some of the high-profile consumer websites and magazines, the fight for a viewer's attention is greater. Therefore, the preciseness of communicating effectively is crucial. Think of it like the water balloon game at the carnival. You have to be on target out of the gate, and steady throughout, in order to win.

When it comes to clever, smart, and memorable B2B campaigns, the percentages of home runs appear dramatically fewer than in consumer marketing. Much of this has to do with a mindset that suggests a business audience is not as receptive to a clever ad as consumer, and therefore, it's more effective being blunt, flat, and straightforward. Could that really be true—that the business audience has no sense of humor, no desire to be entertained, and little patience for anything other than concrete messages? I'm a human just like you are, and I'd give an equally flat no to that answer. People do wear their business hats when looking through trade channels, but the idea that the exclusion of emotion from a business campaign is the norm disregards even the simplest fact that there is no lack of emotion in the average workplace or life. Emotion— whether it's humor, excitement, or a tugging of the heart-strings—is a great starting point when concepting your message. Using it effectively is the challenge.

Take a look at this campaign created for Mediaspace Solutions:

Mediaspace Solutions, originally called Media Space Bank, is a media placement company that handles huge, multifaceted, Fortune 500 accounts for large agencies. It is responsible for placements of ads in hundreds of publications at any given time and in other forms of media as well.

We understood the purpose of what Mediaspace was selling and how and why it's used. We thought that the typical bullet-point-heavy advertising approach so many companies utilized for this kind of detailed service would be unacceptable for this company, particularly when the audience was readers of Ad Age, Ad Week, and Media Week. With some research, we were able to construct a detailed profile of Mediaspace's customer.

The company's average target were middle-management media buyers for large to medium-sized companies or advertising agencies. Their workloads were full, and nine times out of ten, these media buyers found themselves staying late at work managing large-volume placements that required countless calls, ad mechanical reviews, and micromanagement with their graphic production departments. They were stressed out and overwhelmed, and they wanted mostly to get home and see their wives and kids before everyone went to sleep.

That profile gave us what we came to know as the emotional underpinnings of our campaign: Media Space Bank gave customers a break. Although the distinct features of its products and services were important, this was the most powerful reason customers sought out Mediaspace, and it was the best way to explain to potential customers why MSB was built just for them.

We then went about creating a campaign that tapped into the customer's psyche, albeit with a bit of humor. The new company name we created also framed MSB as being that of a supportive "helper" rather than focusing on the specifics of what the company did.

From its first placement, this campaign stood out from the clutter and got noticed. New customers, when they called Mediaspace Solutions, told the company how much they loved the new campaign. That was the company's return on investment. The fact of the matter is that this campaign succeeded not because it was unnecessarily bold. Not because it was racy or loud or different for the purpose of being different. It succeeded because it mixed a clear message that appealed directly to its customer's "need" while also catching their attention in an unexpected way. And that kind of dynamic is not solely the domain of consumer advertisers. B2B advertisers have every opportunity to produce the same type of surprising communication that Apple and Geico, among others, do. Thinking creatively is the first and most logical step. Unfortunately, many B2B advertisers are loath to take it.

B2B Advertising is Too Clichéd

It's said there are seven basic plots in literature that all stories derive from. If so, how can we call anything created today "original"? While the term "original" may always be in question, a better word to describe new work of every form is "fresh." In advertising, "fresh" is always the goal. A unique twist on an old idea is what most good advertising agencies strive for. Still, most of what passes for advertising these days is neither fresh nor original. Although there are few ideas for ads in this world that haven't been done in one form or another, audience's long-term memory is faulty. In that regard, coming up with something unique for your audience is not as tough as it might seem to be, and old ideas can have new life breathed into them with a little twist.

I mentioned my former boss George Lois earlier. George was an old hand at revamping, rejuvenating and adding a twist to familiar concepts. In the late '60s, he created a very memorable commercial campaign for Maypo (an oatmeal product that many readers today may not be familiar with) that included celebrities like Joe Namath and Mickey Mantle crying to the camera, with the signature line *"I want my Maypo!"* Fifteen years later, when that audience was in their teenage years, he revamped this campaign for MTV with celebrities like Sting, Pat Benatar, and Mick Jagger screaming, *"I want my MTV!"* Some of us weren't even sure why that campaign resonated, or why it seemed so familiar, but we were drawn to it out of that vague familiarity. George had done what most good marketers do: take the familiar and make it fresh.

Unfortunately, freshness isn't usually the active word in the B2B marketing space. There are so many clichés in B2B ads that to list them here would take up an entire book. By the same token, many of these tried-and-(sometimes)-true ad approaches do work despite their overuse, and I will explain how. So, without further ado, here is a list of typical ads, and ad approaches, you'll see over and over again in B2B trade:

1. "Introducing..."

You have a new product. You want to give it a coming-out party for your audience. It has a world of new features, is dramatically better than the competition, and screams for advertising that notices these things. Instead, we get *"Introducing the Newest Advance in Accounting Software."* Agencies love "Introducing." In fact, they love it too much. It's old, it's cliché, and you can be sure that there will always be another ad with the word "Introducing" at the head of it in the same publication or site you're advertising in.

2. "The Best (Product Here) I've Ever Used!" [Celebrity/Industry Spokesman Here]

Make no mistake: endorsement ads are important. For some businesses, they drive sales better than any feature-based advertisement possibly can. The problem with most endorsement ads is they feature endorsers known only by industry old-timers and, in a country where youth is omnipotent, using minor to sub-minor celebrities to hawk your wares is about as exciting and substantial as Ed Wood hawking Bela Lugosi long past his prime. Good celebrity endorsements require a solid public relations agency, a budget, and time. If you are unwilling to invest, you should look into another type of advertisement.

On the other hand, if you can find a cost-effective celebrity who fits your niche perfectly and can come across as a surprising choice (like William Shatner for Priceline), you might have something most celebrity endorsements don't—that unique twist that can turn a cliché on its head.

3. "In a World..."

This phrase isn't just the bane of B2B advertisers; you'll also find it in nearly every other action movie trailer you'll see this year. *"In a World of Low-Cost Vacuum Cleaners, Only One Product Stands out..."* The problem I have with the "In a World..." approach is how little it tells you about the uniqueness of the product or service advertised. The intention, of course, is to separate your product from the negative aspects of the competition, but what the advertiser ends up doing instead is giving the viewer the opportunity to question whether this product or service is part of the problem as well.

4. "Does Your Product or Service Act Like This?"

Similar to "In a World..." but potentially more brand destructive, these types of ads usually show the ugly side of a product or service. For example, *"Does your call center connect?"* might show a slovenly phone operator filing her nails while her entire switchboard lights up. The subhead and body copy will usually explain the benefits of *your* call service and how it is different from this exaggerated outcome, but most viewers will be left with a negative feeling, either about the service industry itself or a misplaced belief that your service fits into this category as well (the result, usually, of viewers not reading the full ad—which most of them won't). A way to counter this kind of negative ad is to cut your design in two and make the negative much smaller in scale to the positive.

5. LARGE WORD!

There are very few ads I want screaming at me, let alone screaming something of as little profundity as "STRENGTH" or "ENDURANCE." The big word ad is there to get your attention, and having done a few myself, I know that the approach works under certain circumstances. As I explained earlier, ad design needs to be tailored, on some level, to the design of the competition. In the same way that Kraft, during the process of approving new package designs for its products, will align its new design next to its shelf companions for comparison, you as a marketer need to find out what kind of look will stand out from the clutter.

Furthermore, as long as the message is strong and resonates, you can find yourself with a very successful lead generator.

6. Comparisons

Their product, our product. Notice the difference? Comparison campaigns have been around forever, from taste tests to Bounty paper towels. They are the go-to idea when you've exhausted your first few inspired ideas. The high mark for this kind of campaign was Rolling Stone magazine's first foray into advertising: "*Perception, Reality.*" Directed at their readers (but also at their advertisers) this campaign contrasted the perception of who their audience was and the reality of what they actually really were (for example, the hippie of old was, today, a well-off businessman). Although there is always room for a new twist on the comparison campaign (which GEICO proved recently with their customer "taste test" commercials), nine times out of ten these ads tell you what you already know.

7. The Bullet-Pointed Monster

The best ads, whether consumer or business, focus on one unique selling proposition. Why? Because it's easier for the audience to focus on one message at a time. Most businesses (particularly those that sell products with many features) want to cram their ads with every possible feature, specification, and technical detail they can. The assumption is that they are paying for the ad space, so they may as well get the most out of it. Although this approach is practical for ads that appear in the yellow pages, it tends to diminish the value of the product or service when this type of ad appears in respectable trade publications.

What you want to do with B2B is bridge the gap between what you want to say and what you should settle for saying. You can always produce a campaign instead of a single ad, and use each one of your three or four selling propositions as an individual conversation.

8. "A History of Service"

Ads that tout a company's longevity draw a fine line between promoting experience and casting themselves as old-timers. Whether longevity works for your company or not depends completely on your business. If you're a local company that specializes in tree care, that history might work in your favor. If you're a communications or electronics company, history isn't what your audience wants. Instead, your target customers want forward-thinking companies that are innovative and cutting edge. Very few companies can pull this off: one that did is Mercedes, which ran commercials showing the history of its cars. Unfortunately, most campaigns fail when they try this approach.

9. Inspirationally Vacant

Nothing is less effective than an advertisement with a vague, clichéd image and an equally vague headline. How many times have you seen ad or banner with "inspirational" images, such as hands holding a globe or someone standing on top of a mountain, and a headline like "Moving Forward"? More than you've probably taken notice of. The body copy for these ads usually explain that these companies are forward thinking and on top of their game, but their advertising is as vanilla as it gets. These are the kinds of ads that nobody remembers because they all mesh into each other. To break the cliché, the ad needs to be specific: *How* a company is forward looking is far more interesting than merely stating it is.

10. The Clunky Visual Metaphor

Finding the right animal, vegetable, or mineral to convey the message for your ad campaign is a tough egg to crack for even the best creative mind. More times than not, the visual metaphor used is clichéd and tired. Now, I'm a sucker for any good visual pun, but oft-used clichés, like the missing puzzle piece for example, isn't one of them. This cliché is used to show the customer that the company in question is what the customer needs to complete the puzzle that is their service or product. It's a very tired concept that, like Inspirationally Vacant, will cause a customer's eyes to glaze over.

There are better arguments you can make to show how your product or service fits into your client's needs. Once again, find the specifics that appeal to your client's needs rather than another vague general phrase, and you'll have a better chance of winning your audience's attention. Regarding imagery, the list is endless. Most B2B ads today are developed not with true creative in mind but expediency. As a result, most marketers find their imagery through stock photo houses. The best ones, Getty and Corbis, have some beautiful shots that would cost a ton if you had to hire a photographer. But that isn't even part of the mindset of the typical designer. He or she is thinking "business" and spending more time on the type layout (which is nearly always smaller than 10 point on the page) than on the power of the image they choose. As a result, the same types of images are used over and over and over again. Ask yourself how many times you've seen the following (courtesy 101cliches.com):

1. *Close-up of two shaking hands*
2. *A light bulb*
3. *The tin can phone*
4. *A hammer breaking a piggy bank*
5. *Cheetahs*
6. *Chess pieces*
7. *A mountain climber*
8. *A Swiss army knife*
9. *An eagle*
10. *A signpost*
11. *A magnifying glass*
12. *A group of business people smiling*

13. Scales

14. A dictionary definition

Although clichéd images are sometimes unavoidable on a small budget (where your only option is a limited list of stock photo houses and royalty-free photos), a good message goes a long way in helping you find a better visual signature for your campaign. In addition, most of the above clichés can be turned on their heads with a clever twist and good bit of Photoshop work. Always remember this when it comes to creating an ad:

1. **Your message is most important**
   Your headline needs to cut through the clutter and speak directly to your audience in a matter-of-fact, non-salesy way.

2. **Your image needs to add dimension to your headline and message**
   Most of the images above are considered cliché because they are plopped into an advertisement with little thought other than co-opting the visual message they bring with them. Good advertising happens when everything works together.

3. **Your subhead and body copy should add to what we already learn from the headline and image**
   In short, there cannot be a disconnect between any elements of your advertisement. These three things cannot be developed separately then shoved together.

Lastly, a good advertisement should be part of a larger campaign with an overall theme. Themes are what stay with the customer longer than the details of a headline. Themes reinforce your brand and create an overall umbrella by which all messaging evolves. And the point of a theme? Repetition.

The more you repeat, the easier it will be for the customer to remember.

Many B2B Advertisers Don't Embrace Change

What we hear sometimes from new clients is that they're doing fine. Their business is doing well. Their previous advertising efforts haven't necessarily failed, and their modus operandi have proven successful up to this point, so why buck a trend? Our response is usually to ask why they've considered our services in the first place. Change is difficult, and many companies (even successful ones) don't always see the practicality in doing anything different in terms of their brand (if it exists) or how they are perceived. This institutional resistance is reinforced by legal departments that tend to put the kibosh on any proposal that proves too complicated to navigate through easily. New marketing strategies, which naturally require some form of social initiatives and blogging, are the easiest target for these departments, as both approaches require a bit of trust on the part of the company and a degree of complexity in how they are filtered out to the greater world. Let's face it: if your blogger's articles need to be approved in the same time-consuming process that a press release does, they will never have the immediacy that makes blogging so powerful. As a result, most marketing efforts exist at the margins: a new look for an ad or online work, an updated website look with little new material, trade show material, and maybe a few safe press releases that get easy approval about a new product or employee. In the end, the sales force will continue doing what it always does without the benefit and the enthusiasm that a new campaign has to re-energize them, and everything will be business as usual.

Simply put, a resistance to change today, or any day, is

anathema to a company's bottom line.

Consistency and Repetition Are Everything; Most B2B Campaigns Don't Have It

Create an ad, that's one impression. Creative a brand, you've got multiple impressions. Today more than ever, when a company's image exists in the real world, the digital world, and the trade space all at once, consistency in look and message is paramount.

Some companies tend to view their products and services as unique to each other, islands unto themselves. For example, a company that sells computers to educators may also sell microchips to other computer manufacturers. What tends to happen, especially when several sales units are involved, is that different marketing managers are assigned to different product or market divisions. As such, each marketing manager uses different vendors, rarely integrates with other divisions, and there ends up being very little consistency in messaging and design. As a result, what you have are two or three or four different campaigns that may share nothing in common other than the company logo—if even that.

Smaller companies may experience the same issues due to the lack of a marketing department rather than the expansion of one. These companies usually have one person doing everything. He or she has to manage multiple sales departments or individuals and may receive different messaging from each sales division, thus accounting for the lack of continuity between ads. Either way, there is a component in this process that is being neglected.

In the end, there is a reason we equate orange and blue with the New York Mets, or magenta and orange with Dunkin' Donuts. There's a reason why _"Ideas For Life"_ is found on every single bit of messaging for Panasonic and why we instinctive-ly remember the catchphrase *"What Can Brown Do for You?"* when someone mentions UPS. Consistency. It not only im-prints the memory of your product name on the viewer; it also reinforces the idea that your company is an organized brand that knows who it is.

Many B2B Marketers Haven't Got a Clue About Social Marketing

There is a huge chasm between companies that have used so-cial marketing and have some idea about what they're doing and those that use it for the first time and are completely and utterly lost. Watching some B2B companies navigate through the unfamiliar waters of social marketing is kind of like watch-ing a polite vegan fill up his plate at a Swedish smorgasbord. He has no idea what he's selecting and has little intention of eating it, but if everyone else is doing it, he can't be impolite. For your social marketing to work, it requires knowledge of all the components, how they work together, and what you can expect as an outcome. It requires strategy—and an under-standing of your client. It also requires a mindset that embraces everything current, because nothing is as current as a Twitter post or the speed to which online news organizations push information to the masses.

David Meerman Scott, bestselling author of eight books including *Real-Time Marketing and PR*, offers Eloqua, a mar-keting software outfit, as an example of how a company's em-brace of social marketing as a useful tool has actually resulted in millions of dollars of business. Eloqua's CEO uses Google Alerts in his BlackBerry to inform him in real time of news about his company and the industry at large. One night at din-ner with David, his BlackBerry buzzed, and the news at the other end informed him that one of Eloqua's competitors was just sold to Oracle. Big news, one would expect, but even for Oracle, the B2B pipeline moves much slower than it should. He returned to their offices to see how saturated this news was across the web.

What did he discover? That single item—the alert that the company president had received—was the sole news story on this acquisition. As purveyors of real-time media, he knew an opportunity had presented itself. Within two hours, he wrote a blog post discussing the merger and how it benefits Eloqua's business model. This was an even-handed article. The competitor wasn't disparaged, and the goal of it was to provide a fresh perspective on the sale where nothing else existed. The immediacy of the article paid off. As the news spread, his article was quoted alongside Oracle's original press release. It received thousands of hits and allowed Eloqua to own what Scott refers to as the "second paragraph" of the story.

Eloqua's second move was to blast an email to its existing clients as well as prospects that Eloqua knew were clients of the competition. Surprisingly, many of the competitor's clients were unaware of this new announcement since the schedule for the official press release would not be until the next day or even later. In short, Eloqua was able to capitalize on this news, sway more than a million dollars' worth of business its way, and brand itself in the process as a company that's always on top of things, even during dinnertime. Scott has since branded the act "newsjacking", and made it the topic of his most recent book, *Newsjacking: How to Inject your Ideas into a Breaking News Story and Generate Tons of Media Coverage.*

Unfortunately, most companies don't have the kind of infrastructure to enable their employees, let alone the CEO, to blog or tweet on their behalf without going through a time-intensive gate-keeping process.

Social marketing is all about immediacy. It necessitates engaging in real time with customers. Its enemy is the rigid marketing plan that has no place for it and the company that sees no value in it. Because a portion of your competition fits this rigid profile, it might be time for your company to break the mold. The first step is to do what the competition neglects to do and *own* your spot on the web.

Try this. Search Google and find the most appropriate keywords for your category. You may be lucky enough to grab the best position on page one. Fortunately for many, the competition's sluggishness is your opportunity, and that sluggishness is rooted in a much more damaging mindset—that many B2B companies don't think marketing will help them at all.

Many B2B Company Leaders Don't Think Marketing Will Matter At All

A few years ago, I was an exhibitor at a trade show. It was a successful one. I found three new clients through it. One of them was a large company that needed some collateral work done. Another was an ad agency that was looking for an outfit with web expertise. The third was a mid-sized company that specialized in architecture and home inspections. This company had its own building on the south shore of Long Island and had been in business for 50 years. The current owner was the son of the founder. Suffice it to say, this will very quickly become a familiar tale.

The current owner maintained and grew the business through word of mouth. When he saw the opportunity to be profitable in different areas of his field, he took quick advantage of it (that's how he began the company's architecture division). He kept the business chugging forward by keeping his salaries manageable, his service consistent, and his name on the tongue of every property lawyer in his county (because the majority of the company's work came through the sale and leasing of business spaces). He advertised infrequently in the law journals that were popular for those lawyers and…well, that was that. He had his routine. When he saw some of our web work, he decided it was time to update his website.

Unfortunately, his motives for doing so parallel my story about the vegan at the smorgasbord. He felt obligated to update his website; he wasn't doing it because of any conviction about whether it would provide a benefit. In short, he didn't believe marketing worked. What he failed to realize was that his success was, in fact, supported through marketing efforts. He had boxes full of pamphlets created for every different specialty, and he routinely mailed these out to potential clients… but he didn't recognize this as a direct mail campaign. He collected email lists manually and had his administrative people place them in an Excel file for future use… but he never recognized this as his email push. Like many small businesses that stay comfortably where they are, marketing and advertising are perceived as a waste of money. There is no direct return on investment. Unless a potential client comes to you and tells you he saw your ad or found you on the web (and many do), the money isn't the same as a cost-per-item.

Filtering out your marketing message can sometimes be a slow drip. Large companies know this and invest in it. They understand that the most important thing their marketing department can do is oil the machine of sales. When a salesperson talks to a lead and discovers she's heard of his company, it makes his sale that much easier. Does it always guarantee the sale? There's never a guarantee on *any* sale unless all pistons are working in unison, and even then, it's subjective based on the new company's needs, the economy, and where they are in their sales cycle.

Still, depending on the business, the ROI for marketing *can* be sufficiently more direct. For example, one of our clients is a hair-replacement company that gets a portion of its leads through the online products we've developed—a mix of YouTube postings, keyword marketing, and page-one Google searches. The company receives around 15 leads per month. Because every lead is also forwarded to me in addition to the marketing manager, I can say with certainty that 80% of them are people either looking for the company's service directly or looking to include it in their own salons. Given the reasonable rate we charge to them per year to manage their social marketing and website updates (and given that their products start at $5,000), the money this company has made from our efforts is pretty considerable. Marketing DOES work. But if you don't believe in it, and if people like me cannot convince you otherwise, then that, as they say, is that.

CHAPTER 4:

B2B Tools and Strategies — and Methods to Generate Leads through Them

Before you can run, you learn how to walk. And before you can walk well enough to run, you have to know where you're going so you don't go headfirst into a pole.

Part of the success of a marketing plan these days is in understanding the benefits—and drawbacks—of the communication tools at your disposal. Most marketers we know feel the need to try everything and see what sticks. The problem with that approach arises in the lack of attention to some media channels and the abandonment of any structure that could initiate the use of correct channels like a well-targeted scalpel.

In this chapter, you may find some of the programs, strategies, and media outlets helpful in reaching your customers and others completely useless. Every media plan should be as unique as your company or product is.

Equally important is understanding some of the intricacies of the programs and applications you'll need to use to make your marketing plan work. This is not solely the purview of the Creative Director: I've always felt that any good designer, marketer, copywriter, or account person cannot be fully effective unless they also know the benefits and drawbacks of the tools used in creating good work.

Although there is always room for innovation if you have the budget for it, most clients expect their agency (or their in-house advertising departments) to avoid quagmires in the production and implementation of their marketing materials and online initiatives. If you are the type of client or agency that wants to create something unique in the digital, dimensional, or video space (like many large consumer advertisers do in the commercial space), the real question you need to ask yourself is "Do I have the time, or money, to play around and experiment?"

Most B2B clients would tell you no. To avoid racking up costs in areas like these, it's best to get a general understanding of some of the skills usually left for programmers, animators, and editors. In doing so, you will afford yourself the time to experiment within your timeframe and budget—and very likely come in under budget for your efforts.

Getting Started: The Most Important Tool— The Marketing Plan

It may seem elementary, but many companies overlook this crucial step. In order to understand what you want, where you want to go, how you plan to be perceived, and how to get there, you have to write it down.

Marketing plans can be 50 pages or 3. They can include a full media plan or a suggestion of what sites, publications, and events need attention. They can set agendas for quarters or the entire year. What you'll accomplish in writing down your marketing plan is clarifying your goals, thinking through your product or service categories, and pinpointing how you want to spend your money. Most marketing plans include the following:

1. Who is your target market?

Age range. Sex of primary customer. Income level and profession. Education. Location. Luckily, most companies know the profile of their buyers—and knowing your customer defines how you advertise to him or her.

2. How well do you know your product or service?

What are the similarities and differences between your product or service and the competition's? Do you have unique features or benefits? What are the key selling points? We always ask the same simple question to our clients, and most of the time, they do not have the answers on the tip of their tongues. So, right now (or when you have a pen or keyboard available), try writing down an explanation of why someone would want to buy your product and do business with you. When talking about unique features, try to explain them in plain terms. Many B2B products and services are technically complex. Whether or not your customer is an engineer, it's always best to find the easiest, most conversational way to describe what it is you produce.

3. What is the demand for your product or service?

What products or services are popular and which ones need a little push? Based on a product's or service's yearly gross and increase in revenue, most companies have some idea where they want to concentrate their advertising. Most of our clients have multiple products. The marketing plans for these products are based on the following:

• If this is a new product, when will it be ready for market? If it's not a new product, what are the expected profit goals for this product in the upcoming year?

• When are the most important (and well-populated) trade events for these products? For some of our clients, the most important yearly event is NAB (the National Association of Broadcasters). They premiere all of their new products at this event, which occurs in April. As a result, most of those clients' marketing plans must be completed by the final quarter of the previous year so early PR, trade show advertising, and displays can be readied by the event. After the event, their salespeople are armed with the proper materials (brochures, either print or pdf; web links; promotions, etc.) to help their sales, and the advertising campaigns are rolled out based on buying variables for each of their eight markets.

4. Who are your competitors?

What are their strengths and weaknesses? How lucrative is their business today? Do you intend to go head-to-head with your competitors in the same publications and online venues they do? Or are there other strategies, or markets, that the competition has ignored? Is there something your company can promote or enhance that the competition won't, such as exceptional service, or is there a new innovation you will integrate that is guaranteed to make you the shiniest object in the bowl? In this area, doing a little research on your competitors is important. It will give you an insight into what's actually working for them and what isn't. If you have sales people or distributors outside of your company, now might be the time to create a Q&A for them to find out what *they* need in order to sell your product or service better. We've done these, and you'd be surprised at how candid distributors and sales associates are. You may find your strategies changing from putting money into sales materials as opposed to advertising or vice versa.

5. **What is the marketing environment and how is it affecting your sales?**

The psychology of your customer is of primary concern when the economy is in dire straits. You need to research *who* is buying today, and that may determine whether your advertising is focused across all markets or a few in particular that are showing growth. Also, in a global economy, you need to know which countries are good customers. For example, some of our clients have found themselves investing in India and China, because growth there is booming.

6. **How much is your marketing budget?**

Although budgets vary, most marketing budgets are approximately 9% to 13% of annual revenue. It's a good place to start, but smaller companies should be aware (as explained in Chapter 3) that you get what you pay for. There are many creative ways to work with a small budget, but you can't expect to get a five-month banner ad saturation on Squidoo.com, an article in Fast Company, and a robust online presence for a small budget. Spend appropriately. It will pay off.

What's important to know with your budget is how and when your clients buy. Some markets make purchases all year round. Some have cycles. For example, education institutions tend to make their purchases in August prior to the beginning of the school years. Governments begin purchasing in force after the approval of their yearly budgets, which usually occurs around October. What a good media manager can do is find the right site or publication and form a media plan based on these buying periods.

What you gain in mapping out your marketing plan is a way forward with your marketing agency or internal department. By knowing where and how you want to spend your money, you will spend more time following your instincts and getting the most extensive coverage, rather than jumping into publications and events fast and sloppy and missing important opportunities to spread your unifying, consistent message across all necessary media.

What Are The Particulars?

Most marketing plans have one or more of the following:

1. *Online advertising*
   (banners, keyword marketing, page takeovers, videos)

2. *Print advertising*

3. *Smart devices*
   (mobile phones and tablets)

4. *Social marketing*
   (blogging, forum postings, RSS feeds, linking,
   immediacy monitoring)

5. *Web presence*
   (company sites, micro sites, social marketing sites: Facebook, Twitter, LinkedIn, FourSquare, Slideshare, etc.)

6. *Promotions*
   (online and offline, sales-oriented or vertical, which includes a promotion for the sales team and the end users)

7. *Trade shows*
   (displays, printed material, article reprints, branded merchandise or giveaways, event marketing, which could include event organizers or experiential marketers giving your potential buyers a test drive of your product or service, or putting on a show or hosting a dinner)

8. *Public relations*
   (including case studies, testimonials, white papers, and articles about new products, local or national initiatives, company changes that might interest different markets, or useful instructional information)

9. *Sponsorships*
   (maybe you might want to get your company's name on a race car or be part of an affiliate promotion for an event that would complement your company's business type.)

10. *Commercials or industrial videos*

11. *Collateral*
    (brochures, stationery, sell sheets, promotional sheets, forms, etc.)

Not every company needs to or will utilize every one of these tools. Your marketing strategy will very likely narrow down your needs. But there is also a healthy degree of practicality necessary here. If you have a budget of $200,000, you don't want to spend it all in one place (or for that matter, even two places). Budgets, high and low, can be spread around if your marketing is creative. We've had clients who were pleasantly surprised at what we've been able to do with a million-dollar budget, which their previous agency (a huge one) was able to create only an ad campaign, a brochure, and a little PR for that same price. At the same time, a company can't expect miracles with a $75,000 budget if its category is competitive. A smart plan will quell most of these concerns.

So let's take a look at each of these tools in detail: I've numbered them not in order of priority but just as a way to clarify the information I'm providing on each tool.

Online Advertising

According to eMarketer, banner ad spending in 2011 doubled from the previous year. With more banner ads involving video, rich media, and cleverer creative (compared to the ugly, uninteresting, or amateur ads consumers have been used to for a decade), it's no surprise that the cries of a dead medium are premature. That's not to say that this talk is completely without merit. It's true that banner ads (at least the traditional versions, which include the skyscraper and leader boards) are less prevalent, if you take into account their absence on our most popular websites (which have replaced them with text-based ads and rich media offerings for customers); however, they have evolved into something more dramatic in both size and placement.

As a result, a random single banner is not the preferred way to go when advertising in 2012. If your online publication allows it, you should opt for either a "one stop," a page takeover, or, if appropriate, an interstitial:

• A *"one stop"* is when you take over two to three key banner positions on a publication page, usually with your Leader board (728 x 90 pixels—or, if you're lucky, one that runs the full width of the website) the "Boombox" (340 x 250) and possibly a few positions on the bottom. Reinforcing the concept that leaving more than one impression is preferred, this type of placement really takes advantage of that. If you have a clever message and an attractive campaign, particularly one with colors that contrast with (or overpower) the hosting website, the worst you can expect is to seep into the memory of the viewer, even if they don't click.

• *Page takeovers* are dramatic, startling, and sometimes annoying, but they're always attention grabbers. They are usually built in Adobe Flash in transparent background mode (but will very likely be developed in HTML5, moving forward), where elements of the site can appear unmoved, or dismantled, behind the abrupt animation. Takeovers today include video, green screen, 3-dimensional CGI, clever sound mixing and, most important, conclusions that show beauty shots of your product or service. They can be interactive micro sites unto themselves. One thing they are not is boring.

• An *interstitial* is a large billboard ad that appears between pages on a website (or as an opener). The effectiveness of these ads is always in question because they are a clear obstacle for viewers, who assume the article they just clicked on would load quickly. Still, if you choose to go this route, I suggest you ask your online host how long he has his interstitials timed at. If your animation is too long, you may see it cut off before it has a chance to complete itself.

In previous years, the effectiveness of banner ads was measured purely in terms of the percentage of click-throughs based on the amount of impressions the ad received. Given the shift in the marketing industry to all things social, this measurement has undergone a reassessment as well. More advertisers understand that banner ad effectiveness has become more about placement and impressions in the way conventional ads have worked for years. Advertisers have also begun offering new larger-sized banners that are more in alignment with this thinking. Still, although social marketers cry about how that this kind of advertising doesn't work with people anymore (if it ever really did), banner ads will remain a viable marketing option, no matter what they morph into from this point on.

Print Advertising

Some may hear the term print advertising, smirk, and claim it's gone the way of the Yellow-Bellied Seedeater. When you ask them, "Hey! What the heck is a Yellow-Bellied Seedeater?" they'll strike a long look of disgust, and retort "an extinct member of the Emberizidae family of birds, of course! Are you *ignorant?*"

Okay. So you might not get quite so colorful a reaction, but it's true that many believe that print ads—and the print magazines they appear in—are not long for this world. For some clients and categories, that is very much a fact. For others, it's not so cut and dry. It's true that print publications have become leaner and others have moved over to online publishing only, but trade magazines are hardly out for the count. Businesspeople, particularly those in a position to purchase your product, may still be older adults or middle aged. As a result of that, magazines are like comfort food to them. Furthermore, if your competition is actively advertising in these trades, the most likely impression of readers is that your company is not truly a player unless you've got some position there also.

The plus with all of this is that most trade magazines are more willing to bargain with you than ever before—and if you're lucky, you may be able to swing an article mention of your product or service on the page adjacent to your ad. If the publication has a robust online component, you might want to work a few opt-in email blasts into the advertising package. In any event, no one should be writing the obituary for print yet. It's still got the eyes of many decision-makers and a lot more clout than a mere banner ad can give you.

Smart Devices (Mobile and Tablets)

Whereas advertising on these devices caught on quickly for consumer companies, B2B has once again been lagging behind. Much of the delay has to do with cluelessness in how to proceed.

Smart-device marketing for businesses needs to take advantage of the utility nature of these products rather than mulling over where a mobile banner ad or web poster will be placed. While consumers use their devices for everything from viewing the Internet, making calls, playing games, and keeping up with news, business customers download applications that help to streamline their jobs. One of the apps we've proposed to our client includes an ROI cost savings calculator for their engineers as well as a series of how-to instructional videos that educate them on easy fixes and changes in industry rules and compliance. Other companies have developed apps that allow their clients to manage networks remotely, link to communities or networks, and keep abreast of upcoming events and webinars that interest them. Other B2B apps have taken advantage of the GPS chips on phones to direct customers to useful vendors and services in their local areas.

This ability to turn what was previously seen as an entertainment item into a useful business tool is a growing category for the B2B marketplace. Here are just a few examples:

• Oracle's Mobile Assistant gives users the ability to pass information and project management materials back and forth between themselves, salespeople, and customers.

• The FedEx app allows all the same flexibility its website does in processing shipping forms, tracking packages, and finding transit times.

• Xerox thought way out of the box with its app, Competipedia. Knowing that businesses are always interested in the activities of their competition, Xerox developed a wiki-based resource that provides insights and competitive charts on them, including techniques and analysis on how to differentiate your own company from theirs.

Although the current cost to develop this software is considerable given the need to individually code for a number of platforms (iPhone, Android, BlackBerry), other options are on the horizon thanks to responsive web design (which reconfigures your website to function differently depending on the device you display on) and WAPPs (website-driven applications that feed company press releases and news, events, photos, videos, and the like through RSS feeds). Online applications for developing your own Wapps, like Seattle Cloud, offer a series of templates customized for specific businesses and functions. With a little understanding of HTML and CSS, you can be off and running in creating a branded company app usable on all platforms. Still, this is currently a very "custom" business for anything out of the norm, so expect to have a reasonable budget for development, including a separate marketing budget to promote the app, because it will compete with hundreds of thousands of others on the app store websites.

Social Marketing: It Does Work for B2B

There are many books on this subject, written by people in all types of businesses. As someone who has used it in a hands-on way and seen positive results, I can tell you for a fact that social marketing is rock and roll. It's here to stay despite what your parents (or older colleagues) think, and it's not to be underestimated. As with every new medium, it takes marketers some time to figure out how to benefit from it without being either intrusive to their audience or misdirected in their strategy. For many businesses, social marketing is still a mystery not yet solved.

It's curious why so many companies are intimidated by social. If you look at it closely, it's not unfamiliar territory for marketers. It's really just good old-fashioned PR and experiential promotion combined. My first foray into this popular fig of a strategy was way back in May of 2000, when the agency I worked for, Gem Group, was hired to create promotional material for an upcoming TNT series, *Witchblade*. As with everything our agency did, it all began with common-sense thinking. In the case of *Witchblade*, we knew the following:

1. The show was based on a popular comic book developed by a division of Image Comics, known for *Spawn* and *The Walking Dead*.

2.   The comic book enthusiast was an early adopter of the Internet for swapping of images and files and participation in forum discussions.

3.   We had three months to initiate a strategy that would drive online customers to the pilot episode of the TV show.

One of our account people discovered the comic forums on both Image and Dark Horse Comics. As a result, they "joined the conversation" months ahead and became part of the discussion on the upcoming show. We knew at the time that the typical advertising hype wouldn't work in such a setting, so our guerilla marketers engaged with the other comic enthusiasts and tried to characterize themselves as fellow travelers. They absorbed the culture, read the magazines, and became "experts" in the field of comics. As such, their opinions had clout in the forums over a short period of time.

Our next step was to offer an incentive to spark enthusiasm for the show. We did so by offering our new audience the chance to sign up with Warner Bros. and become "Bladewielders." As an exclusive member of the *Witchblade* TV series fan club, they would receive monthly newsletters and proprietary media—games, trailers, previews—that the average person would not find in his normal perusal of the Internet. All this seems pat today, but in 2000, it was revolutionary. As a result of our efforts, *Witchblade*'s pilot episode became the most-watched single show in cable TV history up to that point. To me, this opened up a new and exciting avenue for marketing and one that I've used continuously in all the years since.

In fact, talking about social marketing as a specific category today is a bit antiquated. Social marketing is integral to nearly every marketing campaign, B2B or B2C. What differentiates a B2B approach is the understanding that your audience is small and varied and its needs are specific. Success in the B2B social arena has more to do with a company expanding its customer service arm and offering potential (and current) clients new information, product benefits, discounts, and consistency of message.

For example, in the case of one of our online ventures, HDCameraGuide.com (a site that appealed to the professional camera sales, rental, and broadcast industry), we simply brought the mountain to Muhammad. We created a community and fed industry people useful information. We participated in conversations with them. We offered our opinions on what technology was worth looking into and where the broadcast industry was headed. We made ourselves relevant. That is the sum total of what you need to do with the social component of your marketing plan. Call it added-value. Call it customer service. Call it content creator or whatever you want. The real goal for a business is to find a way to be a destination for those looking for your type of product or service. Any strategy that succeeds in that goal is the right one.

In Social, Manpower is the New Currency

You want to succeed in social marketing? Here's how:

Put in the time.

Social marketing involves a lot of manual labor on the part of the person (or persons) designated for the job. If you don't think an enormous and continuous effort can be made to feed the necessary social marketing channels of your business, you won't get the kind of results you desire. Simply blogging once in a while, posting a few tweets, or creating your LinkedIn profile is not a social marketing strategy.

Think about it this way. Whatever effort you or your team put into tracking down leads is the same volume of effort necessary to make an impression in the digital age. Social marketing, while necessary for promotion, is also an added value for your company. The best way to view it is like you would that potential customer you met with last year, bought a few drinks for, and have been trying ever so subtly to win over from the competition since then. It may take a while, it may require some work, but in the end, your perseverance will pay off. Run your social marketing campaign properly, and you will have that dynamic with several potential customers.

Before we delve into the particulars of each social marketing application, take a good, hard look at your overall marketing initiatives in the digital space. Do you have a respectable site? Has it been updated in the last few years? Have you cultivated any relationships on the web, and can they be further explored, even if you've been negligent? You may be closer than you think to an online strategy...or you may need a complete overhaul.

Social Network Mainstays

Unless you've been working 60 feet underground in a ditch in Northern Alaska where there is not only no Internet access but very little to eat, you've probably engaged in some or all of the social network sites I'm about to discuss. If you're in a corporate environment, your company probably just started talking about using these tools for business two or three years ago; however, some forward-thinking firms (like IBM) have gone further than others. Although I won't go into the depth of detail you'll find in books dedicated exclusively to the subject of these tools individually and technically, I will give you an overview of some of the key initiatives you should take and what you might expect when you become a social-savvy company.

Facebook

Are you familiar with Facebook? Just kidding. The largest social network on the web may not seem like a must for business, but given its reach, it is a foregone conclusion that you will have to consider it. At the time of this writing, Facebook has over one billion active users. For businesses, this application allows you to create accounts, groups, and "Like" pages where marketers can post promotional material, press releases, and videos.

How to use it:

For every marketing program we've constructed or product-specific website we've created, there has also been a Facebook component. HD Camera Guide is a good example of how best to use this application: every time we post a new video or article on the website we create a short Twitter-like link on our HD Camera Guide Facebook page. These posts appear on our homepage and within the homepages of friends and potential customers who have pressed the "Like" button for your business. In addition, we've provided links to the HD Camera Guide blog, and we upload new videos to our Facebook video pages. Once you create your Like or Friend page, you can join groups that parallel the interests of your company. For example, if you are a company that sells green products, there are several groups and pages that support and promote this same type of business. As a result of joining, others find you and become fans of your company page.

Promotions and call-to-action posts are another great way to drive traffic from Facebook to your website. You could upload a current case study link that forwards back to a short submission form for lead generation.

Facebook has also been a great venue for talking to potential customers. We've had countless chats with interested cinematographers and filmmakers on products we've advertised and, when applicable, have forwarded these leads on to our clients. In addition, a third of our promotional traffic comes from our Facebook account. Because our promotions require opt-in email information, we've been able to profile and match our Facebook friends with our website customers and create reliable lists. Facebook also has components that allow companies to create lists of Events, Forum Discussion boards, Photo galleries, Blog, Twitter, and RSS news feeds, as well as its own internal instant messaging system so you can talk privately to your friends and customers.

If you can find a programmer who works in advanced HTML and JavaScript SDK you can customize your web page to look unique. Since most B2B companies are not making an effort to do more than a standard Facebook page, your ability to be ahead of the curve can show dividends with future potential viewers.

LinkedIn

LinkedIn is an absolutely spectacular B2B tool and is essentially the business version of Facebook. In addition to enabling you to quickly connect to your business contacts, their contacts, and their contact's contacts, you can meet other potential vendors and clients through useful groups, find out who has viewed your profile (and, in turn, view theirs—a very handy way to get your name into a potential client's cerebral map) and follow the updates, requests, and tweets of those you wish to do business with.

How to use it:

LinkedIn is only as good as your participation in it. You can feed press releases into it from your blog, post videos, add tweets for professional friends to follow, and, if you don't have an existing website, you can link a URL directly to it. It's also invaluable in terms of discovering connections between potential clients and yourself. Sometimes, the best way to get the ear of a client is to field an existing connection, and LinkedIn allows you to find that connection.

Once you start using LinkedIn, you need to consider it an extension of your business card and outreach. For example, if you attend a trade show, it would be beneficial to "connect" with every one of the potential leads you met there (or whose business cards you received) in order to maximize their recollection of who you are.

The Company page here is key. There are two drop downs at the top for Overview and Service. Overview should contain a one-paragraph description of your company (anything more will not be read) and a link to your website (which will also appear in your right-hand bar). The Services drop down gives you ample room to add substance to any service or product you offer—and, if the rest of your company is properly connected, a direct link to the person in charge of each division (or your sales staff, broken down by region or state).

Another great benefit comes through Recommendations. Getting current clients accustomed to providing you with a customer testimonial in your Company profile carries caché, because LinkedIn's application is considered to be one of the least manipulated on the web. (Sure, you can exaggerate on your case studies a little bit, but don't be surprised if some previous client calls you on it.)

Like Facebook, a user can stay connected to your company through the Follow Company button. This way, all your blog posts, articles, and news will appear on their homepage feed. With 'Profile Statistics,' you can keep track of how well-traveled your LinkedIn page is and make adjustments accordingly. Also, unlike most social marketing websites, LinkedIn actually lets you see who has viewed your webpage. This can be both a plus and a minus. Although it does help you introduce yourself to people who might otherwise not have any knowledge of you, unless you log off before you view profiles, those users will be fully aware of your interest in them. If you intend for that result, fine, but it's probably best to be discreet before you look up an old girlfriend or boyfriend on this service.

Lastly, you are only given one chance to approach a potential link friend. If he or she turns you down, you will not get another chance. To avoid this, it's best to link with all your good business contacts first, your secondary contacts (who you know will accept you) and, by the time you get to a potential client who's slightly out of the circle, that person may consider you if you have a few people in common, which you very likely might at this point.

Twitter

Twitter is not going away. Given that many people have short attention spans and few of us have a lot of time to search for information we need (either for research or decision-making), Twitter is like stepping into a library of ideas in short, camera-ready sound bites. Much of the problem with businesses and Twitter is, as usual, lack of strategy before jumping in. The fact is that your customers *want* information about what you do, what your product does, and how it's all being used, but they don't know that they want it from you yet. As a result, your strategy is to decide what kind of Tweets you're going to major in. For businesses, this breaks down as follows:

How to use it:

You can use Twitter in three different ways:

- **To establish *Thought Leadership***

  Do you have a reservoir of valuable advice to impart to customers about your product or service? Can you speak clearly and deeply about your financial business, or recommend which stocks to buy or what to look out for in the coming year? How about architects? Are there new rules and regulations you can help potential customers with? New materials or styles that may be cost-effective for them in future projects? Are you a political speaker who knows the history of politics and how certain movements have overlapped in the last few decades? Can you cull together a series of outside articles from others that you feel will be of interest to your audience, even though they've not been created by you?

  Being a Thought Leader on Twitter is as much about your audience getting a "feel" for how you think, what you like, and how helpful you are as it is about promoting you and your product/service. Like most of what is successful on the web, free information and advice (particularly when it fits the "theme" of your Twitter strategy) endears you to your customers and potential customers. Like you, their time is valuable. The fact that you've spent time, effort, and thought on your business and can impart your ideas, theories, and tips for free is an extension of customer service is many client's eyes. And because most of us will not become pundits or experts sought after by CNBC or Fox, our best bet at convincing our audience that we are "experts" in our field is through a constant and consistent campaign of Tweets and article postings.

- **For customer service**

  Delta Airlines, as well as many other airlines, has

transported part of the customer service department onto Twitter. The mindset is that Twitter is the new customer service "chat" function—and rather than having to create an option for your website that functions on all browsers, operating systems, platforms, and mobile devices, why not just co-op Twitter's ability to "answer" your questions through Tweets? In Delta's case, the Twitter account is live and active. Other companies tend to use their accounts to update clients on the status of their service. This can work as well for large communication outfits like Verizon in alerting customers to potential problems, disruptions in service, and upcoming changes as it can for a construction company letting its community know about deadlines for government paperwork and things to look out for in its projects, houses, or buildings during each of the seasons.

- **For market research**

There is no better way to find out what your competition is doing, saying, and thinking than to peruse their Twitter accounts. In addition, where applicable for particular businesses, Twitter can be as useful as reviewing forums and chat rooms on what clients are saying about you or your business. The great benefit of this tool is that, like a personal blog, you're able to see into the mind of those who are tweeting. You can also get a sense from some potential clients whether they are searching for your service, growing, shrinking, or if they have something in common with you that you might be able to benefit from when you're trying to get in the door.

Flickr

Flickr is an image and video-hosting website. It grew exponentially thanks to its compatibility with blogger software and the ease-of-use for which bloggers can post their photos and embed them into their websites. Flickr affords users many options, from posting large, high-resolution photos to adding text, links, and keywords to accompany them. Users such as photographers and graphic designers have used their Flickr accounts to show their portfolios.

How to use it:

Thanks to its high ranking in a Google image search, Flickr has become a must-use application for companies, particularly those that sell or promote products. In addition to driving web traffic through standard means (sites, PR, guerilla marketing, Facebook, and Twitter), Flickr is essentially a "back door." How many times have you done a Google image search, clicked on the image, and found yourself on a site you normally would never find in a typical search? For those of us looking for particular products, services, or even sometimes people, it is a spectacular way to dig through the clutter. Moreover, Bing (much to its credit) has tried to build part of its search engine on the power of image searches over text searches. It's a practical approach, given our proclivity to visual stimulation and the extra power an image has to drive that next click.

I suggest you duplicate your site images (and video) on your own Flickr page. Give it the same name as your company or site, if possible. Add a keyword-rich description and title to it, and a specific link (rather than a general link for your website). We've had websites that have received the bulk of their traffic through a popular Flickr image. In addition, every time a user co-ops your photo for their website your blog, you reap the benefits in your Google ranking, because that's yet another sticky link that will move you up in the search.

Google Plus

Google's answer to Facebook, Google Plus launched in 2011 as a more "public" social marketing format. The architecture is similar to Facebook: Friends, Family, and Followers listed on your right, a blog-styled content area in the middle, and the beginnings of spaces for groups and companies to gather (called Circles). Given Google's reach, and the fact that Google Plus's content will be indexed within its search engines (Facebook's, of course, is private), this application screams out for B2B companies' participation.

How to use it:

According to Frank Isca of Weidert Group, a Wisconsin marketing agency, Google Plus has, in its short lifespan, become an SEO magnet for content shared by businesses and brands. Given that it's part of the Google umbrella, this is hardly surprising. Just like the immediate benefit you get by applying Google Analytics to your website (a Google robot searching your site quicker than if they had to find it), Google Plus company pages will naturally show up near the top of a search for your name. Although that alone is hardly a reason to join, the caché of being listed within the Google network itself is a benefit to your SEO in the long run.

What it means for businesses is that Google Plus needs to be high on the list of social marketing absolutes when putting together your strategy. In November 2011, Google Plus unveiled "Pages" which businesses can use to build their profiles. With Direct Connect, another related service, your brand can be found through a proprietary search that locates only businesses with the "+" after it. Once you've created a profile, the way Google Plus works best for business is through "Circles." When you and friends, you now have the options of "categorizing" them. What you do is simply click on the connected ring icon on the top bar. All your current contacts will appear, and a series of circles with breakout categories are shown. The first circle allows you to create a category of your own and drag the appropriate friends into it. Once you've done so, you can privately share content that is business related in that circle to either inform your category or try to open up discussions.

Google Hangouts, on the other hand, allow you to have direct conversations with others in your circle. With a live webcam and use of extras (such as shared notes and sketchpads, document integration, and screen sharing) you can create your own webinars (which you can also time-schedule) or video conference calls.

On the far right of the application homepage in the users information is the icon for "+1." This function is a way for users to rate information found across the network. Given that it functions in a very similar manner to Google's search hierarchy (where sites that are found to be more informative than promotional rank higher on searches), there is the possibility that this function might increase a company's search position. Also, although Google reported in July 2011 that it would deliver business-based profile pages within a year, it can only benefit to get your company on the map early. Even if you discover that you may need to duplicate your information on a "Business" page, you will be ahead of the curve by creating your profile now and becoming familiar with the software.

Slideshare

You've just created a webinar or presentation. You've spent many thousands on it, and you've used email blasts to drive traffic to it through lists you've also spent money on. Overall, it was a success. Now what do you do with it?

You will very likely post it on your website for viewing and download. If you really want a bang for your buck in terms of SEO, you should also post it on Slideshare. Slideshare is a social media site, but only in the most general sense. It is used primarily by businesses to post presentations, bookmark and tag them, and allow other users to comment. Like LinkedIn, you can join groups and interact with interested parties.

How to use it:

Like Google Plus, Slideshare content shows up strong in the search engines. Despite having a wide reach, Slideshare is not the kind of service Jay-Z will be using to promote his new album. It's not a consumer application. (You might, however, find him posting a presentation for one of his other businesses.)

Slideshare is perceived as a B2B channel, and the majority of what you'll find there are company presentations, educational material, videos from trade shows, seminars, and industrial product overviews as well as eBooks. Although you should certainly consider it as one of the sites to use to drive traffic to your content, it is also a great place to post short-form PowerPoints that address single questions your potential customers may have. By answering them in a unique, colorful way on a PowerPoint (and including your branding and contact information), you manage to turn a simple answer to a business question into an authoritative piece. Adding the right keywords to accompany it makes certain that the same question posed on a Google search will bring up your Power-Point answer high in the ranking.

Pushing Your Content Out Through Social Discovery Websites

Having content on social sites is a good start. Making sure

they appear near the top of searches for this content is even better. Pushing them out through Facebook, LinkedIn, Twitter, Slideshare, and others is par for the course. Your next step is to gather your content and push it out to a broader audience that is actively looking to read it right this minute. For that, you will need to use a social discovery site.

Social discovery websites are less formally constructed news or blog portals; instead, they're fast-moving content highways. The goal is to get your new article out there, have it appreciated and shared (or "dug" or bookmarked) and, as a result, open it up through popularity to a wider audience within the discover network. Every link from these sites goes directly to the hosting website rather than a being hosted by the site itself (as a press release would be).

What follows are the three most popular discovery websites. There are others as well. Because reach is just as important as targeting your content when pushing it out on the web, I would also recommend any other site like these that can do that.

Reddit

With traffic of more than 15 million per day, Reddit has exploded in popularity since October 2010. Like all discovery websites, Reddit allows you to post articles of interest, which can be commented on and shared. Reddit users who view it are encouraged to vote up or down, therefore contributing to the ranking of the article in their directory. Reddit has a wide variety of categories, from technology to science to WTF, and top-tier tabs with lists of what's new, controversial, and hot.

Digg

With traffic of more than 4 million per day, Digg is taking up the rear on Reddit. As the result of a site redesign in 2010, which had a few bugs and also changed the algorithms for how pages benefitted from votes (called "diggs," of course), it went from being the leader in the category to a follower. Don't let that stop you, however, from using it. Digg is a more robust and colorful site; it's free to join (like Reddit); it has a wide variety of categories that are easier to find (Reddit's navigation is a bit industrial); and it has buttons, such as the Digg Newsbar, that can be easily installed at the header of your own browser as a constant feed from the website.

Delicious

With a new redesign befitting HTML5 compatibility, social bookmarking website Delicious (formerly del.icio.us) has an attractive user interface and a clear method of "digging" through content based on categories and likes. In addition, its Link Checker Tool enables you to see how your own website is faring and who (if anyone) is bookmarking your website, and it provides instant feedback on how you should move forward in your social strategy if your content is not being seen.

Stumbleupon

Rather than requiring that you to go to its website to recommend content, Stumbleupon provides you with an easy-to-use browser tool that allows you to bookmark your company's press releases, articles, and the like. Stumbleupon boosts page ranking, is a good analytical tool for your social strategy, and has a cost-effective paid placement network where one in twenty "stumbles" (searches) are websites that have paid into the advertising system of the company. According to CEO Garrett Camp, Stumbleupon "refers almost as much traffic as Facebook."

Strategies for Discovery Websites

Discovery websites require a committment from you or those in your company to give them value. With Digg, Delicious, and Reddit, it is encouraged to have as many people in the company create an account and spend a designated portion of their time pushing company content through the sites. Be aware, however, that most of these websites can tell quickly if your intention is merely to push your own content and not contribute to the overall goal they have of promoting content the users really like. One way to get around this is to make sure to recommend links that are outside of the realm of your company's interests. In the past, I've created accounts in all these directories, and for every digg or ping or stumble I make to my sites, I do six more for other interests. That way, the community wins, your goal of promoting your company above all else is not as blatantly obvious, and good articles and press releases don't get penalized.

Trade-Sponsored Email Blasts

Over the last few years, trade publications have diminished. What was once a vibrant channel for B2B marketers has folded, due to dwindling advertising revenue. The smarter trades have strengthened their online components and still carry weight in their industries, not just as thought leaders but also due of their most valuable commodity: their lists.

Targeted email lists are as valuable as gold to B2B marketers and, whereas yesterday's advertisers exploited those avenues through direct mail, the new strategy is to rent them for trade-sponsored email blasts.

I'm not referring only to advertising in a trade channel's newsletter (which I do recommend). Instead, I'm referring to an option that most trade channels either have or could easily offer: the trade-sponsored individual email that is built for single clients.

With an opt-in list and an email that is "approved" by your trade partner, you are much more likely to reach qualified respondents than if you just buy a list and take your chances. In addition, many of these publications produce email blasts around important trade shows and, particularly if you are participating or showing at one of these events, having an email blast reach a potential customer with the header like "IndustrialHeating.com: ASHE Conference & Technical Exhibition: New Heater From Smith Manufacturing" will help you break through the clutter much easier than without the publication's permission.

What's important in the production of these blasts is that they are colorful, are direct, and link to a specific page on your site (or an accompanying site) where you can collect the customer's data.

For example, with Canon, our agency spends a good portion of its energy every year creating promotions around its largest trade shows, such as NAB and InfoComm. Through trade channels such as Broadcast Engineering and TV Technology (both of which had robust online components and large email lists), our agency created product emails, added a promotional element to them, and invited potential customers to visit Canon at its booth and receive their benefit. If the promotion wasn't built around a trade show, the strategies remained similar: introduce a customer to learn about a new product or service, and provide a link to discover more. Or produce a video to make the introduction entertaining—and incentivize people to offer their contact info.

Keyword Marketing

Keyword marketing has grown more complex over the past 10 years, and although the prime positions for valued searches aren't yours 100% of the time as in the past, the increased level of traffic makes the point moot anyway.

Developing any keyword campaign involves a combination of knowing the tools, understanding the options available to you, and forming a strategy that takes advantage of your budget, whether it's small or large. Google AdWords is the 600-pound gorilla in this room. This service has the ability to display your ads nationally as well as locally. In addition to the text campaigns most of us are familiar with that appear at the top and right-hand side of a search, there are also image ads that show up on Google's Display network. Many high-quality websites use the Display network in their AdSense accounts (where clients can add Google's advertising to their websites in exchange for payment based on click-throughs). Because display ads outperform text ads by 300%, it's best to have both in your plan.

While the strategy you use in your AdWords account must vary based on your business, the following has proven useful in terms of cost and effectiveness.

Research Your Keywords

Thanks to Google AdWords Keyword and Traffic Estimator Tools, you can take the few words you're already familiar with as big searches for your category and find many more that are equally as good or better. Google's keyword matching tool will identify dozens of words, including their traffic and costs—and don't neglect the names of your competition! Some of the best click-throughs my campaigns have received came from individuals searching for a competing company and finding my ad either above or to the right of it.

Create Several Headlines, Descriptions, Keywords, and Groups of Keywords in Your Text Ads

Spending all your money on one or two ads is not a practical way to use this service. Search involves variety, and creating several combinations of ads based on all the criteria your audience searches for will also give you a better idea of what ads work and which ones don't. For one of my clients, a hair replacement company, one highly successful ad has the title "Most Natural Hair System." With a click-through rate of 2.09% (which is great in search percentages), it far outperforms the expected searches such as "Hair Replacement" and "Going bald."

Google AdWords, along with Yahoo and LookSmart, are the most popular do-it-yourself keyword ad programs.

Spread the Wealth

Don't put all your financial eggs in the basket that includes the most expensive and general keywords. Find combinations and highly targeted ones that can also contribute to your bottom line. For example, you may want to put a substantial amount of money behind click-throughs for the term "printer ribbons" if you're a company that sells these products, but you should also spend on keyword combinations like "Epson printer ribbons" as well. You may discover that your most successful search terms are also some of the least expensive.

Spreading the wealth also involves putting part of your keyword budget in Bing's and Looksmart's applications. Their network not only reaches places that Google's doesn't, but you could discover that the same terms within their network yield better results for less money.

Put a Substantial Amount of Your Budget Upfront

This has been a successful strategy for my agency for years, particularly in combination with a product launch and press release. If you have an average budget of $3,000 a month for one year, I suggest doubling it up on the front end (first three months). What it will do is get you more impressions and earn you more chances to appear in out-of-network blogs and websites. When these sites are indexed by Google's search robot, your ad might be picked up as well. When this happens on websites that are not searched as regularly, it gives you a sticky link for at least a month that may help push you up in the organic search.

One trick of the trade involves your daily limit. Although it may seem practical to set a daily limit of $30 a day for a budget of around $1,000 a month, the reality is that you will be charged that amount only if you receive enough click-throughs to justify it. To account for this limit, Google will average out the amount of impressions you receive during a day. To improve your impression numbers, you might try quadrupling the daily limit. That way, with daily monitoring of your account, you can be certain that you will receive four times the impressions you would have and will more than likely get closer to hitting that actual $30-a-day mark. If your ads prove to be more popular than your budget allows, you can progressively cut back on the daily number as the month proceeds. (Bear in mind that this strategy requires daily monitoring of your account to ensure you don't blow your budget and overspend.)

There are other options to choose from within all these services, including demographic bidding, ad rotations, and varying the landing pages on your site with individual ads.

However, it's the effort you make in managing your campaigns, getting rid of ads that don't work, and reinforcing those that do that will increase the number of click-throughs to your site and make for better leads.

Other Ad Networks

In addition to AdSense, there are other ad networks you can run your display and text ads through, including:

1. **Adnetik:**

By aggregating data through relevant sources across the web, Adnetik claims it can competently target your media to an appropriate site or blog better than its competition can. Adnetik reads millions of URLs and classifies them based on their brand equity, safety to the brand in question (i.e., whether there will be opposing articles on you, the client), clutter, and the quality of the content. According to its site, Adnetik claims the highest conversion rate and lowest cost per action (CPA) of any of the competitors it has come up against in recent case studies.

2. **Tribal Fusion:**

Claiming to represent only the highest-quality websites, Tribal Fusion secures high CPM rates for its advertisers by targeting their ads in the most valuable spots, while also aggregating top high-traffic sections of much smaller websites. As a result, an advertiser gets prime real estate on websites like Rollingstone.com, Dictionary.com, HealthGrades.com, and others. Tribal Fusion specializes in rich-media ads and hosts a variety of ad sizes, including pop-unders, which apparently carry a high CPM rate.

3. Commission Junction:

If you plan to sell your product through an e-commerce website, the big fish in the pond is Commission Junction, created in 1998. Its clients include many of the top 500 retailers. Many clients manage their placements through CJ's proprietary software, but the company also has a division that will handle all the work for you and provide you with monthly result surveys. Although there is no downside for the advertiser in working with CP, wannabe affiliates do have to submit an application. Due to the popularity of this service, it can be difficult for some to get accepted into the service.

CHAPTER 5:

Your Company On The Web: Being Specific About Your Brand Online

An online presence today is more than just a company website. An online presence is multifaceted. Depending on what your company does and how much time your audience spends using digital media, your ability to find your customers—and engage them—in several places at once should be a primary goal.

Being large or small makes no difference. I have a friend who sells a single product (roof vent motors) and has a keyword marketing campaign, two e-commerce websites, and a presence in Alibaba.com (where he gets the majority of his leads), TradeKey.com, and a host of other sites, directories, and forums that are specific to his business. All provide reach as well as the leads and, while he continues to pursue traditional methods of selling his product (e.g., by telephone), his ability to be ever-present in the Google search for "roof vent motors," among other categories, is vital to his success.

The first question you should ask is what kind of site you want, how it should be built, and what components are important to ensure search engine popularity. In addition, you need to consolidate how your brand will translate across the web. Will your website be an online brochure or a robust, ever expanding information portal that engages its customers as well as reaches out to them through other channels? While your business model will influence the latter, here are some suggestions on how to build the right site with the right tools and make sure you're in the best possible position to take advantage of your marketing strategies now and in the near future.

What Should We Think About Your Company's Site?

A B2B company must have a competent, well-designed, professional-looking website. Some of you may argue on the issue of what "well-designed" is (and there is certainly some value in the argument that content should rule over design); nevertheless, a poor or mediocre site design says something about you and your company that you'd rather not have said. A poorly designed site gives off an air of disorganization. An old site suggests you're too lazy to update, and your business methods may suffer from the same. An amateur-looking website, or one that is too lean, presents you as a lightweight in your industry.

Not wanting to foster any of the above impressions, I suggest you look through the best websites in your industry (and other associated industries) and strive toward that kind of look.

It may require you to write more about your company than you plan to initially, but get used to that. All new marketing channels require homegrown content, and lots of it. It may require you to have someone other than your brother-in-law's son who just graduated with a degree in JavaScript coding to design and build said site. It will most certainly require *your* attention, if you are the company owner and/or marketing manager, because most impressions will develop from this first or last visit from customers, no matter where they come from initially (your blog, your Facebook, or LinkedIn account, etc.)

What kind of site should this be? That's a different question altogether. If you are a consultant or service company that needs customers to understand what you do and what value you bring to the table, a blog format might be your best bet. Otherwise, you may want something that outlines your company and a Twitter link to provide your current and potential clients with your wisdom. If you sell industrial products, it can't hurt to have a website that provides company information, user testimonials, product descriptions with features and specs, and a live person to talk to should an imminent sale come from the web. (This is as simple as setting up a live chat that particular salespeople can be designated to use. For some of the Live Chat software, responders can be forwarded to individual email or text-messaging software.)

Whatever website style you choose, your site must continue to reinforce your branding look. Remember, a brand provides companies with multiple impressions. The more consistency you have in your brand look, feel, and messaging, the more likely potential customers will be to recognize you (and if they attend trade shows, they will recognize your booth branding as well).

The Mechanics of Making Your Web Presence Known: SEO and the Important Circle of Three

Before we get into the details of building a website that will position your company at the top of the search engines (and function well for your future sales initiatives), it's important to discuss the three most important components your site must coordinate to ensure your Search Engine Optimization runs smoothly. These are your domain name, website header title, and your homepage content. Connect these three components through keywords and a consistent SEO strategy, and you will be well on your way to securing good footing with that 800-pound gorilla of search, Google. While it is not the only thing that will bring you up in the rankings, it is a must to get you started.

The Importance of Domain Names (Plural)

There are several things you need to concern yourself with when choosing a domain name, and none of them has to do with your company name. Unless you own a company called Baseball Mitts and Baseballs, and unless you can or already have purchased the domain names "Baseballmitts.com" or "Baseballs.com," your company name is probably the least likely keyword that customers will use to find you on the web. Chances are also pretty good that there will be a domain name out there that suits your company just fine, even if you have to use the word "co" or "corp" at the end of that name.

Purchase Keyword Specific Domains

In addition to finding your company website name, you should also find other domain names that complement the keywords you find most vital to selling your company's product or service. For example, if you sell avocados, you may want to invest in the keyword *guacamole*. A good domain name might be guacamole-avocados.com. If you are a physical therapy service, you might want to invest in a domain name that includes the words orthopedic or rehabilitation.

For one of our clients we created *SteamBoilersForHospitals.com*. For their education market, we purchased *SteamBoilersForColleges.com*. Another client, a large lumber yard in NYC, wanted to dominate the search for "green lumber," so we created *GreenLumber.net*. Your best bet is to do a survey with existing clients and ask them what words they would use to search for their product.

The simple truth is that your web presence today is more reliant on a multitude of components, sites, social networks, directories, and placement in vital searches than it is on the "power" of your company name (unless, of course, your company is IBM or Apple, and even those companies are building their presence toward specific keywords rather than their corporate names).

Matching with your Website Header Title

Once you purchase your domain names, the next important task is "matching" it with your header title. The header title <title>, which will be located in your website's source code below <html> and above <meta>, are the words you see at the top of your browser above your link. This is also one of the first things Google's search engine will index, and it's important to make sure it works diligently for you.

Google loves websites with consistency in subject matter. And there is nothing more consistent than a site with the domain name buttonsandbeads.com and a header title that reads Buttons, Beads, Sewing Material even ahead of the company name. Website titles should also contain at least a few of the keywords crucial for your search. We've followed suit with this strategy for every single one of our client's sites, and they have consistently found themselves competitive in Google searches.

After the company name, list other services or keyword combinations. For example, GreenLumber.net had the following title: "Green Lumber—Green building products, Green leeds, NYC East Coast Supplier."

Homepage Content

Whether your website is large or small, it is important to have some kind of homepage content that talks about your company in a keyword-rich manner. Sure, Google and Bing have nothing more than their logo and a search window, but they function on a completely different level and are a different type of site altogether. Whether you have a company website, microsite, product or service-specific website, or industry-focused website, you'll need to marry your keywords through some public content (the header title is hidden and the URL is, of course, a different animal entirely). All you need to remember that this is a content-driven medium at its core, and the more you have to say, the more others will have the chance to read what you have to say. In doing so, don't forget to sprinkle your message with the words and phrases you think people will use to find your site.

Make sure your metatags and meta descriptions complement your title and URL:

This is old news here, but you need to find at least 10 important keywords to list and come up with a solid, 35-word keyword description. After the title and URL, this will be the third place the search engines will index.

Place Google analytics code on all your web pages:

Google's search spider will eventually find your website and log your information in, but why wait? By registering with analytics, you get an automatic bump through their search apparatus. Every time my company did this with our market-specific sites, it got us recognized in the search within hours rather than days and, for a short period of time, appeared at the top of the search without too much extra work.

What to Look For in a Hosting Space

As far as most companies are aware, hosting space is just the location where their company website sits. They rely fully on their programmers or IT people to handle the complex maze of operating systems, programming languages, and name servers that appear to be too technical for the average worker to fathom. For some companies like Oracle or Microsoft, yes, they would be too complex to get involved if you're not already someone who writes C++ code in his or her spare time. But for the average company, buying a hosting space and building a website is much easier to understand (and even handle partially on your own) than you know. What most people don't know is that the majority of the programs they need to create robust sites, blogs, e-commerce apps, and forms are all available when you pay your yearly fee. You just have to know what you're looking for, how much flexibility you want to have, and what software applications you think you'll need to get your site up to date and ready for its marketing or sales push.

Whereas the largest companies have the money to start from scratch with programmers, most smaller or mid-sized companies would find such costs beyond their range. Designers who are trained in web interface software (such as Dreamweaver and the now downward-moving Flash) usually push their infrastructure issues out to straight programmers and coders.

For the marketer, this is all just technical gobbledygook. It doesn't have to be. What follows is a clear path for non-programmers to get a site up and running for their business, including information on what kind of software they should look into and what strategies they should consider.

Although hosts are abundant, what you really need to look for is the ability to expand with ease and little extra cost. I usually pick hosting companies that include a range of shared servers (which host thousands of websites from different vendors) and dedicated servers (single servers, or partitions, that host your website or websites alone). The reason for this is two-fold: if you host a client that uses a small shared space for its website and decides to expand (either by making efforts to increase traffic or adding functions beyond the scope of the current space), you can simply upgrade your service. On the other hand, if you have several clients (or one client whose traffic explodes), then a dedicated server fits the bill well. It allows you an enormous amount of flexibility in handling traffic (that doesn't interfere with shared clients) and the ability to manage site upgrades that previously could only be handled by the host company itself. From the hosting site control panel, you can also create email accounts with ease, check site traffic, block spammers, manage multiple domain names, and create backups.

Like most programs today, the interface is user-friendly and easy to navigate. Unless there's a good reason to go with a huge, robust, proprietary server (or your client is a company that hosts its own website), I generally look for a hosting company that offers Cpanel or Plesk as its interface, and includes either Fantastico or Spectaculous. These are packages of web applications, tools, and functions that are popular across the Internet. They are also easy to set up (just a few small steps).

There is no necessity to get involved in manually creating databases, uploading information files, or dealing with shell scripts (a method of installing software that only hardcore programmers seem to know).

Installation is simple. Click on the Fantastico or Spectaculous button. You'll find a new control panel window with a generous list of content management systems and ecommerce software, including Drupal, Mambo, Joomla, and Magento among many others. Under the blog listing, you'll see install buttons for WordPress and Nucleus (I'm a WordPress fan), among others. Want a blog? Easy. Click on WordPress. Pick the application you wish to use and press the button.

The domain will be listed there. What you'll do at this point is decide where you want the site directory listed—either in the root (which is the main area of the website that corresponds directly to your URL) or in a separate folder for the application to be housed (for example, with hdcameraguide.com, we have a folder called "guide" where the application was installed. Therefore, the direct URL to the website is "hdcameraguide.com/guide").

There is a benefit to using a separate "directory" rather than the root. First off, if you want to delete or remove the entire site outright, you can grab that solitary directory folder and be done with it. Second, if you stick with it, it provides you an opportunity to gain another keyword you may not have in your URL. For example, our website, *betterbusinesspresentations.com,* has its website in a directory called PowerPoints—the keyword of the majority of work the company produces and one of the one of high value in the search engine.

Next, chose the username and password you intend to use. Press install. In a few seconds, your bare-bones website, with all the power and possibilities Wordpress or other applications can afford you, will be ready for use. Bingo. You've just saved yourself a few thousand dollars or more, and you can now use that money on other valuable commodities like photos and videos for your website. Unless, of course, you want to have your site built from the ground up.

Building Your Website: Custom or Out-of-the-Box

Ask a hard-core programmer whether he believes a large company website should be built with existing software and templates or be coded from scratch, and you won't lose any money betting on the latter.

Whereas many companies rely on their IT departments for advice on what direction to go in building their sites, the answer will usually come from a combination of necessity, practicality, and timing. The usual argument from your programmer will be that an out-of-the-box solution isn't as customizable (which depends completely on what your company wants to accomplish with your website) or is too code heavy or "W3C invalid" to be used in the first place.

W3C stands for World Wide Web Consortium, an international community that works together to develop standards for the World Wide Web. It's good practice to have your websites built in "clean" code, which is similar to saying you shouldn't write an essay with misspelled words or questionable grammar. But unlike an essay, the viewer does not see code and although we can agree that a company site should be as error-free on the invisible back-end as possible, it is not a game-changer when it comes down to the most important player in the game, Google. According to Matt Cutts, head of Google's webspam team, historically Google has not punished websites that do not conform to the strict codes of W3C. Much of this has to do with the fact that most websites do not conform to these standards, and to single them out would mean singling out the majority of websites. To counter this, Google claims to rank websites based on several criteria, including rich and remarkable content, metatags, and compatibility with a wide variety of browsers, and, according to Cutts, "We don't give any boost in the ranking to pages that validate."

In the end, the choice between building a brand new, custom-coded company website or using what's called a Content Management System should not be predicated on whether that site is fully W3C standard or not. Get the best programmer you can find, and hopefully the compliance issues will take care of themselves. In addition, developing with an out-of-the-box solution will still require the work of a programmer, who will more than likely make sure your CMS works just as well as your custom. What's more important and the sole purpose of the company website is for it to be accessible to those who are looking for it and ranked well for those who are looking for your company's particular service or product. With that in mind, let's look at the types of website solutions that exist for companies large and small.

Content Management Systems (CMS)

A Content Management System, or CMS, is what most companies, large and small, use today to create their websites. This application is a server-based tool that allows the user to create dynamic, multi-functional websites where the actual web pages are built out of "modular" elements. Modular means that everything is built separately: content pages, menu navigation, sidebars, footer content, etc. As in Microsoft Word, you have a wide variety of functions to choose from and, after getting past the small learning curve, most find these-user-friendly programs far more effective and rich than the old way of building site pages individually, through programs like Dreamweaver.

In addition, most of these applications have diverse functionality that include lead-gathering databases (which can be downloaded into Excel files), newsletter capabilities (if you have a hosting space that can accommodate that), and page-specific SEO and keyword plug-ins that allow you to customize every part of your site to work best for Google searches.

There are literally hundreds of CMS systems, but I'm going to concentrate on the three most popular free ones (Word-Press, Joomla, and Drupal) and the three most popular paid versions (Expression Engine, Moveable Type, and Ektron).

WordPress (free):

If you intend to create a blog-like website (or, for that matter, a blog), you can't go wrong with WordPress. This program is by far the most popular of all CMS systems and is used by amateurs and professionals alike. Found on most hosting sites as a free install, WordPress is a cinch to use. Right out of the gate, you are given a choice of three templates, but there are dozens of sites that sell custom templates, and uploading them to the application can be done in a few easy steps.

What I like most about WordPress is its search engine friendliness. Google loves this application, so there are never any worries (as there are with some programs) that technical mumbo-jumbo on the coding end will prevent the search engine spiders from indexing your site properly, therefore sacrificing search positions that are should rightfully be yours.

What I don't care much for is the difficulty in molding these templates into uniquely structured sites. If you're not much of a programmer, you're likely to be stuck with the standard blog look that everyone and their mothers are familiar with: large left-hand content column complemented by a narrower right-hand column with navigation and links. If you've got a brand look that doesn't fit that architecture, you're in for several weeks of programming to get you where you want to be. Also, in blog format, if you intend to allow commentary, you'll find yourself fending off dozens of spammers once they've found you. It's not unheard of to log in to the WordPress back-end and discover hundreds of spam comments waiting for approval. Although I'm certain there are security add-ons to battle this problem, they're not native to the program, and given that the comment deletion software doesn't allow you to delete everything at once, you'll find yourself going through page after page, deletion after deletion, in a much more manual manner than you'd prefer.

In the end, however, you can't go wrong with WordPress as long as you're flexible about your design, and it's got enough great functions and add-ons that most users have yet to leave it for another application.

Joomla (free):

This open-source CMS is a personal favorite. After trying out several early CMS systems, including Mambo (of which Joomla is an offshoot), PHP-Nuke, PostNuke, and others, I found Joomla to be the best fit for many of the websites I've needed to produce for my clients. Joomla is endlessly flexible, has hundreds of templates of every size and variation available in the marketplace, and, like Wordpress, has a community of programmers who are constantly updating, changing, and adding to the ever-expanding module count. If there is a function you can think of that doesn't exist in the application already, chances are some clever programmer has created it and offered it for a small price or as a free upload on the Joomla extensions website.

In addition, I've found this application to be an SEO magnet. Joomla's back-end website control panel gives you multiple options for formatting web pages, along with access to a community of programmers who are always adding to its functionality.

Nearly every website our agency has created in Joomla has worked its way swiftly up the search engine ranking (with help from PR, guerrilla marketing, and traditional advertising). An add-on extension allows users to customize web page SEO in extraordinary detail, and Joomla's menu options include a variety of different layouts and dropdowns. The only downside with Joomla relates to two issues: one is a minor glitch in the SH404SEF plugin that has long since been resolved on current versions (clearing your cache was necessary after you've made several changes, or changes would not show up later) and the other pertains to the limitations of its expansion (if you intend to create an endless portal with hundreds of right- and left-hand modules, you will eventually hit a wall with this application and not be able to produce new ones).

However, unlike WordPress, many of the security issues have been worked out of the Joomla 2.5 and beyond, its templates are HTML5 compliant, and Joomla is not going anywhere anytime soon.

Drupal (free):

Drupal is stable, scalable, and is known to be relatively trouble free. It is considered the number one free choice for creation of online publications given its high page count. If you're planning on creating a large online magazine, this might be your best free choice (Joomla, as mentioned above, hits a wall with some of its options when your module numbers are too high).

Unfortunately, Drupal is not as rich in templates and plug-ins as WordPress and Joomla are, and if exploring endless choices of designs (over many years) is part of your modus operandi, you'll be plum out of luck with this CMS. Nonetheless, it has been around a long time, is extremely scalable, and can handle heavy traffic. In addition, its streamlined code (built mostly in Javascript and CSS) keeps the application very SEO friendly. Sony, AOL, Warner Bros., and The White House have all run websites or components of their own larger sites on Drupal.

Expression Engine (paid):

Sony, Disney, Cisco, Warner Bros. You name it, they use Expression Engine. Built on open-source PHP (much like the freeware listed above), EE is a commercial service that offers enormous flexibility and unlimited potential to create whatever type of website you desire.

The user interface is extraordinarily friendly, and a non-programmer will need only minutes to get up and running on creating a site. With multiple management features, you never need to worry who has access to what on the back end.

One of the benefits of a paid system is a support team for security issues. In contrast, with a free CMS, you and your programmer are essentially on your own (with the exception of troubleshooting forums). Because Express Engine's staff gets paid a salary to make sure all your technical issues are resolved, that takes some of the worry out of the equation.

Moveable Type (paid):

It seems that many a blogger, once successful, moves over to Moveable Type (MT) from WordPress. Unlike WordPress, MT allows the customer to manage several blogs or websites all at once. Like WordPress, MT is open source, but it also has a sales-based component that larger companies gravitate toward. Created in 2001, MT is written in Perl which works natively with the popular MySQL databases. (WordPress, Joomla and others are combinations of PHP and HTML language). The latest version of MT also allows users to change themes with relative ease—a feature that other programs (including Word-Press) find to be admittedly more difficult.

Ektron (paid):

With companies like CitiGroup and Microsoft buying into Ektron CMS, it's no wonder Ektron is at the top of the list for paid CMSs. One of the benefits of this system is that it is also a DMS (document management system) that allows you to edit your online documents in any program you wish, including Microsoft Word, Adobe Acrobat, and more. It also has a built-in ecommerce function for those companies that need it. Its library of supported apps is limited, but custom widgets allow an enormous amount of personalization. Still, at a license cost of $7,200 a year, it's a major investment for some companies, especially when the ability to do everything and more is still free in the open-source versions.

Custom-Produced Websites

Here's the skinny on building a custom website from the ground up: If you have a great programmer/designer, he or she will be able to create something no one else has (some CMS website designs, just out of expediency or sheer laziness, are rarely unique). For example, if you want your website to look like a donut where the copy blocks appear in a circle around it, you can do that. You can do almost anything you want. Furthermore, if the code is written correctly, it will be clean and easy for Google to search. When updates occur, they will also be built to W3C web standards, and you can tell everyone you know that your website is the best example of the artistry of programming known to man.

Now, will it make one iota of difference to viewers who visit your site whether the programming is HTML5, CSS3, PHP, or ASP? No. They will not care. What's more important to your potential customers is if your website is easy to navigate through, quick to load, and has content they want to read or view or listen to. Everything else is secondary.

That said, there are some great new HTML5 websites that have been built from scratch by talented programmers. These sites are winning web awards all over the place and are linked to by potential customers and admirers alike. What is also true is they will probably cost you an arm and a leg to produce if you decide to go that route. Large companies often do. If you're not a large company, the other options have already been presented to you.

The One Thing Every Website Needs to Have on Every Page: a Lead-Generation Form

Name. Email. Phone. Company. Submit. You can also include a test area for the potential client to ask a question. You can offer free advice or a free case study. You can promise a discount if people contact you online. It's really that simple. Put it in the upper right-hand corner on every single page of your website.

There is no mystery to generating leads from your website and, even though the book *Inbound Marketing* suggests your Contact Us page is the lowest-converting call-to-action you can create, you will still need it. Customers look for it. Three times a week, one of my clients, a high-end hair manufacturer whose products sell for several thousands of dollars, receives leads like this from its Ask a Question page:

> *"Hello, [Your product] seems really promising. Do you have any locations or affiliates in Los Angeles? Thank you."*

My client produces hair replacements for direct customers and also franchises the service to salons. Each month, there is an equal amount of leads from customers who want the service or want to make an appointment, and customers who wish to include it in their salon. They all come from the Contact Us page. My client produces videos, has an aggressive keyword campaign we manage, and a website chock-full of information. Still, when it comes down to contacting them, many potential clients use their Contact Us page.

There are many books out there that spend several chapters on Lead Generation forms. I'm not going to do that, as there are several ways to generate leads through the methods suggested, from promotions to social marketing. Leads will come. The question is whether your sales team will follow up on them.

The One Thing Every Website Should Have but Doesn't: a Live-Chat Function

Live-chat software is abundant and most of it works the same way: You sign up for the service (or you can install it: Fantastico and Spectaculous have a great program, Help

Center Live, which is an easy install from your website's Control Panel). Then you add your email to the application, create a button that leads to the user interface and place it on your homepage, and then leave the application open on your desktop while you're working. If someone wants to chat, you'll hear a familiar "ping" (just like Instant Messaging), and you're off and running. If you can't be at your computer, most applications have the ability to ping your phone. If you simply don't want to be reached, it will automatically tell potential customers that there is no live person and they can leave an email message.

Many companies don't take advantage of this option because there is no one on the sales team who is the designated "chatter." Their fear, of course, is that customers will become enraged if there is no Live Person and that will affect the company brand. Companies know their clients best, so if they're pretty sure a majority of them will turn green and growl "Hulk smash!" if they can't reach someone immediately, I'll concur that a simple email form would suit them best. For others, it's just another option to make available that lets your customers know you're open for business.

The Future of the Web is Here in Responsive Design

For every company out there who appreciate the previous suggestions I've offered but want to look further into the future for the next step of online site creation, it's time to talk about Responsive website design. Consider this little nugget: According to a Microsoft Tag study done in 2011, the majority of web users will migrate to their phones by the year 2015. Given the popularity of tablet devices, doesn't it seem to suggest that companies will need to modify how their websites are built, in the near future? Or will every company need to pay to create a website, an iPhone app, a Blackberry and Android version of that app, and a tablet version of all of these things?

Not necessarily.

Responsive design sites are built to look like regular websites...until you reduce the size of the browser. Then, thanks to some remarkably clever coding, they reposition themselves (links, dropdowns, art, copy) to fit the dimensions of the device they're viewed on. Ethan Marcotte, who first proposed the idea of a flexible, malleable multifunctional design in May 2010, suggested this new dimensional design. It wasn't until the middle of 2011 that the design layout began to catch on (in addition to the appeal of the cost differential of not having to rebuild your presence every time a new platform gains popularity).

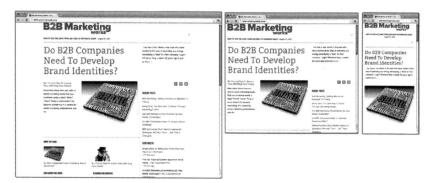

Responsive design allows your website to appear three different ways until it hits "stress points" (pixel dimensions of the browser) that force it to reconfigure. In short, if you are flexible with your website's appearance, have an audience of potential customers that spend more time mobile and less time in front of their laptop (which, in very short time, will be the majority of us), designing your website with these accommodations in mind might be the best way forward. At the very least, it will ensure that you won't be rebuilding your website yet again in another few years, like you've done in the past.

Creating a Blog and Getting It Seen (and Read)

As mentioned earlier, blogging is hard work, but no harder than creating a category-focused portal (or anything else, for that matter). If you are committed to blogging and have something to say about your business, here are some steps you need to take to get your blog seen and read.

For this form of communication as well as others, you need to choose a domain name that includes your keyword (or keywords) and/or the breadth of your subject matter. Once you've begun the process of building your blog site, you'll need to do the following:

Claim Your Blog on Technorati

Technorati is a search engine for blogs. It is the most well-known resource and an absolute must to be recognized as a blog with standing. Along with Blogged.com, BlogCatalog. com, and BlogSearchEngine.com, it is a quick and easy way to extend the reach of your currently unknown writing. Although it will take some time (and a good deal of content) to work your way up the list in these sites, being the 50th most popular blog is really not a necessity. What's more important are the links because, like everything else, it's how you appeal to the Google search engines.

Find Other Blogs in Your Business Space, and Comment on Them

Part of the job of getting recognized in the blogosphere is by talking to your audience in venues off-page. Every business category has some forum or meeting place online. Become a known quantity there. Help others who ask questions by being the expert. Make thoughtful comments on subjects that matter to you. Include your email as a reliable source for information about the industry. Do ALL of this without shilling for your product or service—not yet. The reality is that as long as you are coming across as honest, helpful, and insightful, readers will eventually be open to hearing about what you have to say outside of that particular forum. So, when a subject comes up that's appropriate, you can direct your readers to an article you've written that addresses their needs. If you can, you might try to entice them with a first paragraph followed by a link to the rest of the blog article. Now, how will you get others to find your blog when you're not directly talking about it in other posts? Include your URL in your signature. Either display a graphic or a direct link. If you have proven yourself as a reliable source for your industry, you'll find those links used and traffic being generated by the strength of your reputation.

Create a Flickr Account and Build a Database of Images for Your Blog

Suppose a potential client is looking for a piece of medical equipment you happen to sell. There's a good chance that for this type of item, people will likely do an image search. Flickr is the top image- and video-hosting website, and the strength of that position, along with your blog post about that type of product, may be one of the best ways to get yourself on a Page 1 search. In short, if you are not on Page 1 for a direct Google content search, you'll want to hedge your bets and use Flickr to its full potential. Create an article, embed your Flickr-hosted images and videos in it, and make sure your Flickr images also have descriptions and links back to your article. On one of our blogs, 20% of our traffic came from only two images.

Invite Guest Bloggers

Arthur Germain of Communication Strategy Group (mentioned in Chapter 2) takes full advantage of his blog articles by producing variations on their subjects as a contributor on other industry sites. One of them, Business2Community.com, looks for leaders in the B2B industry to provide content for its website, and Arthur is happy to contribute. Many industries have similar collaborative or group blog models, whether it's for politics (DailyKos.com), education (EdWeek.org), or engineers (Engineerblogs.org). Like becoming a consistent commenter, being a guest blogger can also help you build a following that you can capitalize on.

Find Articles in Major Newspaper Websites on Your Subject and Comment

Google's search engines value links in high-valued websites. One of the best ways to make sure you're represented there is by commenting on articles that reference your business. If you are able to include a link there (or provide a link back to the high-valued site in your blog post), you will be well on your way to letting Google know you've got content to contend with, and that will help further your rise to the top of the search.

Make a Habit of Linking Your Content to All Your Social Channels

LinkedIn, Twitter, Facebook, YouTube, Pinterest, Reddit, Stumbleupon, Delicious, Digg... every time you create new content you need to make your other audiences aware of it. Giving these audiences a way to read your post on your blog is equally as important as the blog itself.

Create a Press Release on an Important Post

It may seem like overkill, but a press release through eNewswire.com or PRweb.com will increase your reach dramatically. As mentioned earlier, it will also provide countless links to it (many sticky) and will allow other bloggers who haven't found your article already to include it as content or reference on their own blogs. If the cost for paid PR sites is too expensive, try FreePressReleases.com. I have articles from this website that are still referenced four years later.

CHAPTER 6:

Unique Ways to Break Through The Clutter

We've talked a lot about digital products you're already familiar with. Now let's talk about a few you might not have thought about.

Many are under the mistaken impression that a company website is the only valid location to direct potential customers to through all their off-page marketing initiatives. The fact of the matter is that many customers show up at your company site once having already become familiar with you and *sold* on you at one level or another. One of the best ways to have them discover you is for them to read about you, your product or your service somewhere else—preferably on the kind of website that caters to your business. While PR has been responsible in the past for placing articles and reviews in reputable magazines and trade websites—and blogging has opened the door for your company to push content out to the masses—there is no reason you can't create a trade channel of your own to do the work for you. That's what we did by creating Category-Focused and Market-Specific websites for your clients. The results were surprising.

Category-Focused Websites

Let's say you're a customer looking for accounting software. You have no experience with searching for something like this, know nothing about the features, and have not been given advice on any companies to pursue. You are, essentially, starting cold. Many of us find ourselves in this position daily because it's difficult to obtain referrals from friends or associates for everything. Having done this before, you know instinctually what your next move will be: You'll hop on your computer, phone or smart pad. Your browser opens to Google. You type in the words "accounting software" and get a list of results. The question now is: Which listing catches your eye and what does it tell you? Lets take a look at the results:

> Sage Peachtree **Accounting Software** Program Solutions
> www.peachtree.com/
> Sage Peachtree is a network-ready **accounting software** system for small businesses under 50 employees. Save time and money with Sage Peachtree.

> **Accounting Software** | Business **Accounting Software**, Systems
> www.redwingsoftware.com/rwssn/?page=329
> Business **Accounting software** to manage finances. Make important business decisions and increase profitability with CenterPoint **Accounting Software**.

> **Accounting software** - Wikipedia, the free encyclopedia
> en.wikipedia.org/wiki/Accounting_software
> **Accounting software** is application software that records and processes accounting transactions within functional modules such as accounts payable, accounts ...

Sage Peachtree? Redwing? You may not know these companies. However, they are on Page 1, and for most of us, that carries a bit of clout. You'll probably choose one of them to review and be on your way.

But let's say you're a great accounting software company that is not listed on a Page 1 search: what options do you have to pull in this valuable Page 1 business? Let's see: the cost per click on the keyword "accounting software" is astronomical, so that's out of the question. The URLs for "accountingsoftware.com" and "accounting.com" have been taken for the last decade, so unless you have five to six figures and a strong-armed guy named Bruno, you'll be plum out of luck in acquiring those prime domain names. You could create a Facebook account, but there aren't a great many out there who are dying to "Like" your accounting software page, especially when most of the public is unaware of you to begin with.

What you could do is create a Category-Focused website. Call it a review site. Call it a guide. Call it an information hub. Whatever you call it, it won't be your company site, but it will end up working harder for you. For most online searchers, the company site is where they go if they've heard of you. If they haven't, your best bet to grab their eyes is by creating a source for all things accounting. We've created these sites in the past, and there is a reason this approach works that can be explained in five simple words:

Google Loves Information-Based Websites

Company sites, which are essentially long-form advertising vehicles, are not the most valued commodities in the Google search engine. For sites that have no internet presence, have not advertised, or sent out press releases, or saturated all the accounting software online and offline publications with advertising and articles, their chance of gaining position for high-valued keyword or keyword combination is slim.

What is always of value to Google are sites that provide unbiased information on a particular business, service, or practice, and provide information and links on a wide variety of products or services within a category.

Think about it. What do you almost always find on Page 1 of a keyword search? A Wikipedia listing for that keyword. A "review" site for those products or services ("10 Best Accounting Software Products"). And what kind of site is the customer for these products likely to view if he's unsure of what's out there or wary of being sold to? Not your site on page 32, but, likely, "Accounting Software Reviews" at positions 1 to 3. And, believe it or not, your chance of getting a top position as a Product Advocacy website grandly outweighs the chance of having your company site grab that position.

One of our agency's clients had products that sold to a very specific market. There were only a few online communication hubs for these products and a couple of large, well-known publications. As this client's advertising agency, we had a great relationship with these publications, advertised constantly for these clients in those publications, and could generally get more for our advertising dollar than someone else might. But still, we had to pitch the publication on articles. We had to wait until an issue that focused on our client's products was in the works (if it was) before we could get the greatest benefit out of the advertising we paid for. We had NO control over the whens and hows of doing work with these publications on any basis. We couldn't publish content about my client daily or weekly there. Every time we looked to send a specific message to the publication's opt-in lists, it cost our client an arm and a leg. So, instead, our agency created this Category-Focused website. It was a "Guide" on the products that my client's product was built to work with.

Building It for Google

In deciding what the Category-Focused site would be and how best to build toward Google compliance, our agency laid down a few ground rules:

1. The site would be an unbiased, non-sales-focused "information" hub.

2. A third party would run it.

3. All the products my client's product was compatible with would be represented and in detail, so the site would be perceived as a thorough source.

4. Competitors would be represented as well, and the site would refrain from criticizing them.

5. My client would get the best-positioned ad banners. In short, this was how the client really contributed to the site. Advertising revenue, not very different from what they were getting through the other trade pubs in the industry.

For their money, my client also received several well-produced videos on its products (which were intermixed with videos about its compatible parent products) and an application that narrowed down a customer's product with the right one from the client.

In short, my company created the kind of publication that the client would naturally advertise in and sponsor. The unbiased nature of it appealed to customers because they were not being sold to or deceived. And because the site was an information-based website, Google and other search engines were more friendly to it, and an entirely new world of promotion opened up for the client, in terms of getting eyes on this new and unique entity.

While originally built to give our clients an extra venue to market in, HDCameraGuide.com has, thanks to a robust social and SEO campaign, become a well-known resource in the broadcast camera category.

So what happened? Within the first month, the "guide" went from 0 to 2,500 unique visitors. Three months later? 10,000. Six months after that? 39,800 a month. It also happened to attract the EXACT customer the client was looking for. We were able to update information, products, and trade show videos on a daily basis and in unison with campaign launches. We could sponsor promotions that targeted the client's customer needs and, in addition, we found ourselves with extra revenue from those companies that our client sold their products to. And, as a general resource, we found takers on Facebook, Twitter, YouTube, and a WordPress blog as accompaniment to the guide's brand. At the time of this writing, we have 6,400 Facebook friends, who we update daily on new products, videos, and press releases from the site's subjects and our clients. On top of that, we are even sourced as a reference in the Wikipedia listing for "digital movie camera."

There were other benefits as well.

Since our guide offered promotions, member-specific videos, and case studies, we were able to gather our own opt-in email list and marketing information about these members. We could clue them in early on new product releases, invite them to view podcasts, and offer one-on-one discussions with our client's product developers and their users. We also sponsored videos and FAQs with valued members of that business community and took part in forum discussions about the industry and its components.

All in all, it proved to be one of our agency's most valuable assets in marketing for these clients. Given its creation as a free resource, it luckily took on a life of its own and, to date, is as well-known as some of the industry's top trade channels.

And it all started as an out-of-the-box solution to a B2B problem.

Market-Specific Websites

I'll make an educated guess that for some of you out there, your product or service is sold in more than one market. You and your company know these markets, but the question is whether you've had the resources to tap into all of them. Also, with a smaller budget, you may not have had the opportunity to explored avenues other than trade ads and banners.

One of our agency's clients sells industrial boilers to large institutions. After a sit-down with the client to discuss marketing for the New Year, we found out that two of its most lucrative markets were in education (to universities and colleges) and medical facilities (to hospitals and research centers).

Our agency had already produced several case studies and white papers and had ads running in all the right trade channels. But, except for the client's website, the client had little to no extended online presence.

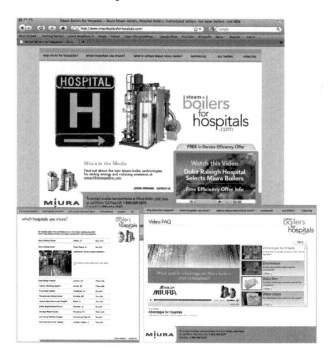

Market-specific websites allow companies to compete for organic keyword positions their company site may not be built to accommodate.

So we got to work. The first thing we did was ask this question: What were the popular terms that hospital and university engineers used when searching online for our product? Answer: *"Hospital steam boilers." "University steam boilers." "Campus boilers."* As a result of our research and the positive numbers we found on them, we moved ahead with production of their first online market-specific websites—this one geared toward the medical industry. We filled this site with market-focused FAQs, videos and case studies, product information, and contact forms that forwarded directly to our client's emails.

What surprised us most after launching it was how unique this approach was for the industry. The competition as a whole wasn't even considering this type of strategy. Sure, a few of them had paid keyword campaigns and supportive dealers who spent a pretty penny shilling for them online, but nobody was taking advantage of the organic search in the same way we were.

The lesson here, of course, is that specific keywords don't need to be relegated to the bottom of the AdWords budget. Traffic may be slimmer for those searching *"hospital steam boilers,"* but you can be sure they are also more targeted. On the web, like elsewhere in life, experimenting with something new can often times be a winning investment.

CHAPTER 7:

Launching Your Online Campaign to the Power Of Three

Our category-focused and market-specific websites didn't accidentally show up on top of the Google search. Their traffic numbers weren't due to some lucky article that captured the attention of the entire industry they focus on. Their ascendancy was the result of a very disciplined campaign strategy that guaranteed dividends as long as we made sure every line item was met. Your strategy might need a longer cycle (and some of our other launches have, depending fully on what the product or service was and their online market saturation), but, for us, the planning and execution of our launch has always been multiplied to the power of three. What does that mean? Here's the formula for the first three months of our online marketing campaigns in a nutshell:

- Three new articles or new content pages per month
- Three new press releases a month
- A three-month keyword campaign
- Three posts a day through Discovery websites
- Three discussions created on appropriate blogs or forums
- Three Twitter posts a week, three Facebook posts a week
- Three newsletter releases or email blasts from your own personal list or trade website lists

By implementing this plan aggressively for three months you are telling Google's search spiders that you are a information website to be contended with. Once they get the gist of who you are and how to categorize you, you'll begin to move up the organic search in a far more rapid manner than a much slower, less structured plan could offer. The whole point of all of this is to go out into the digital world with as overwhelming a force as you possibly can. In addition, the momentum you create will be like a condensed version of what much larger, content-based websites do on a daily basis. Here are the details:

1. **Three new content pages per month**

Google's search spider will only return to your website if there's something new to index. Every new item indexed has the potential to move you up the ladder of the Google search. Think about it. What are the top websites in the world and how many new posts or fresh bits of content do they generate daily? Facebook, YouTube, Twitter, Amazon, Wikipedia, Blogger...every single one of them adds new content by the second. Now, that doesn't mean you should (or can) do the same thing, but it's important that your website has new material on a monthly basis that is not only tied well to your product or service but is keyword rich as well.

2. **Three new press releases a month:**

PRWeb.com and eNewswire.com are your most-valued new media channels when launching a new website. There's no better way to place multiple press release postings across thousands of high-traffic websites (including Google News, etc.) the way these applications do. Coordinating it with your keyword and site launch will help enormously in making your website a success. Also, when thinking about the kind of PR to write, understand that one of your largest benefits will come not from placements in Google and Yahoo News, but cut-and-paste work from independent bloggers that make your post a permanent part of their sites. We want to create content that is sticky, and the best way to do that is to avoid the standard PR articles that most companies put out, which typically pertain to a new product being introduced, a new employee hired, or a new market pursued.

Instead, write articles that offer bloggers something that their audiences will gravitate toward. For example, if you are a software security company, you might write something along the lines of "10 Ways to Ensure Your Company's Web Security." For more detail on this, see the upcoming section on Public Relations.

3. **A three-month keyword campaign**

Not only do we suggest you do an aggressive three-month keyword advertising blitz, but that you spread your campaign dollars out to at least two programs other than just Google AdWords. I've outlined exactly what to do in the previous section under Keyword Marketing. It's a formula we've used before that bears fruit.

4. Three posts a day on discovery websites

Digg, Reddit, and Stumbleupon. There are others mentioned in the previous chapter and you can use them, too. As I explained earlier it is necessary to create more than one account (or have others in the company create accounts) so these sites don't see you as a shill. Discovery websites are enormously helpful in pushing your message out there to audiences that aren't finding it through all your other channels.

5. Three posts a month created on appropriate blogs or forums

As I explained earlier in my discussion of the *Witchblade* TV show launch, much of the buzz generated for the show was enhanced through forum and blog postings. Especially in B2B, potential customers want to hear what others are saying about your product or service. If there is some new information on it, this would be the place to post it. Now, many forums require that you become an active member and participate in several discussions before being given the ability to post your own links. If this is the case in your business category then it's prime time you become an active member and get into the habit of talking to your audience. Later on, when you're a known quantity (and a helpful one, hopefully) your announcement will be received well by these forum audiences.

6. Three Twitter posts a week, three Facebook posts a week

This should be part of your daily routine when releasing new content on your website. The same goes for the release of a video as well (however, this one should include YouTube, Vimeo and all other social video channels). Facebook and Twitter audiences are tapped into these programs constantly and, particularly if you are a company they follow or like, you'll find a steady stream of traffic back to your website by interested parties.

7. Three newsletter releases or email blasts a month from your own personal list or trade website lists

Also discussed in more detail in a previous chapter, newsletters and email blasts are mandatory ways to continue your outreach to potential customers who have showed a prior interest. Trade website lists in particular are the result of opt-in users who, more times than not, have actively pursued having information fed to them. While three a month might be beyond your budget (and your audience may get tired of seeing you in their in-box), make sure to send out at least one a month to stay fresh in the mind of those receiving it.

And we didn't stop there. Both types of websites required a continuous flow of new content and information to keep it situated at the top of the search. In addition, we added a promotional giveaway to the mix that helped push our numbers up further. You see, even for those searches where you're the only contender, competition will find you eventually if there is enough good traffic (and even if there's not).

After three months, our plan tapered off. Keyword marketing dollars were brought down to a reasonable number (and one that could be more easily monitored). Press releases were limited to one per month and email blasts through trade websites were created as needed. All other portions of the plan— forum and blog postings, new content creation, social and discovery website postings—continued in force. The end result is that we've gained top spots for important Google search terms, mentions on more websites than we can count, and a consistent flow of traffic and customer prospects that would have taken us a year or more to cultivate with half the effort.

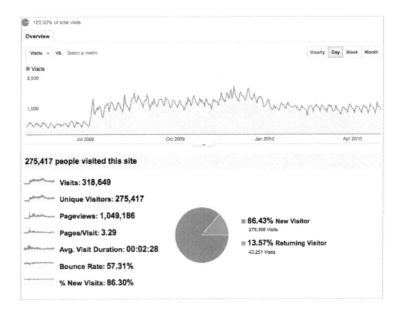

As a result of our "Power Of Three" strategy, HD Camera Guide's visits soared.

CHAPTER 8:

Google Penguin: The Game Changer for Online Search

If you're a business that relies on Google for revenue, it would be surprising if you hadn't heard of Google Penguin, the last algorithmic update from this massively successful juggernaut. Within days of its launch, Penguin became the bane of existence for companies that counted on their search position and the enemy of every sites that benefitted from "gaming" the system through questionable measures.

Let's put it this way. Whether you're building your company's first website or updating your last one, Penguin will define how your company engages the web from this point on.

History

Penguin was created as a software update by Google to decrease the ranking of sites that use "black hat" SEO - techniques that include keyword stuffing, duplicating content, participating in link farms, and cloaking, a technique where programmers hide keywords on a page by giving them the same color as the page (while the user may not see this content, the search engine will pick it up). It was also an attempt to reward websites that provide fresh content daily, stay relevant and consistent regarding their subject matter, and use off-page social networks (such as their own creation, Google Plus) in ways that increase awareness and add to the conversation they're already engaging in.

The update went into effect on April 24, 2012. Hundreds of thousands of websites felt the burn immediately, dropping down or out of key search spots. While sites that manipulated Google may have deserved these just rewards, other websites that never intended to anger the behemoth were also punished. E-commerce sites, for example, were hurt because a great deal of their content, such as product descriptions, features and benefits, were handed to them directly by their product distributor - and duplicated on dozens of sites including their own. What it appears happened here is that Google rewarded the originator of this content (which in many cases was the product's own website) and decreased ranking on its duplicators (resellers and the like). Others that were affected include older websites that, after several generations without cleaning code on legacy pages, contained programming language no longer beneficial with current browsers.

Speculation about how to fix these problems was rampant given that Google never offers update guidelines on how to adjust sites for their search. As a result, it has taken time to get a handle on effective methods for doing so. What follows are some post-Penguin guidelines to ensure your site build or update is effective and your ranking remains robust:

1. It's STILL all about content

Relevant, targeted, original content is still the best way to make sure your site ranking increases with Google. As I've stressed before, you cannot simply re-use the same tired brochure copy over and over again and make inroads in your online strategy. You need to write. Writing must be integrated into the culture of your company or at least one person in it. Otherwise, you'll need to hire a social marketing/SEO outfit to do the writing and the blogging for you.

Furthermore, competing in a Google search is no longer about having text that contains keywords. The quality of the content you create is evaluated on how useful and pertinent your articles are to those searching. Under the *Public Relations* section of *Traditional Marketing Strategies You Should Never Neglect,* I outline several ways to create content for audiences that will not only break the clutter but create a framework for how a B2B company needs to perceive it's content.

1. Become engaged with your audience

It's called "Community Building" and it's more than responding to a few posts. Community Building requires companies to extend their customer service arm into the daily conversations on the web that matter for your business. This is the reason getting "connections", "likes" and "comment threads" are so important through social channels. The more you engage your audience online and talk to them directly rather than create "business copy" for them to read the better your ranking will be with Google and, for that matter, your network of leads. According to Forbes, companies are discovering that their customers are willing to talk about their purchases, the problems accompanying them, online. Engaging these customers will generate good will for you in forums and blogs, add to what Google considers relevant conversation, and help reinforce that culture of social interaction that most B2B companies until recently have ignored.

3. Cut out doing things you know are questionable

Spamming blogs and forums with content just to provide your website link, posting links on websites that have little to do with your subject matter, creating dozens of Facebook pages about the same or similar subjects with numerous links back to your site, and launching "landing" pages that are nothing more than link farms within your company's sitemap. If you, your programmer, or your social marketer are performing "black hat" SEO, you may not have been noticed before Penguin. Suffice it to say, game's up.

4. Get rid of duplicate pages

Does your website still have pages that should have been eliminated years ago? If you've been on the web for a while and have gone through several programmers the chances are very likely. Try Googling your site with this search structure ("site:websitename.com") and you'll get an inventory of every link Google's indexed from your site. At that point, begin deleting and/or changing content on these pages to avoid duplication. Remember: old websites still available for search, old articles referenced through secondary links, and even dummy pages from your content management system you thought were history are all anathema to Penguin.

5. Create a Google Plus presence

Want to *really* get on Google's good side? Create an active, rich, and engaging presence for your company in the Google Plus network. Google Plus, unlike Facebook, is tailored to appeal to business and, if you haven't already noticed, company pages in Google Plus are showing up more and more on search page one. That should tell you something.

5. A few words about keyword density

The new directive in SEO is that your article, essay, case study, or white paper not be littered with any more than 5% keyword density. This is not a hard number. Most pages that show up on Page One searches do not conform to this formula but what is important is ensuring that your new content not be manipulative. Use keywords when you need them but do not write to them. As search algorithms become more and more complex and built to compliment the way human beings think, all of us need to find ways to write that's closer to the way we talk. Given that, it is still my belief that a one-on-one conversation between two people always wins a sale over a carefully written company boiler plate. Your online content should follow suit.

As time goes by, more will be learned about how Google Penguin has changed the game. Inevitably, hackers and programmers will also find ways to crack the veneer and game the search engine despite these new updates. The best approach is the same approach I've laid out before: content-rich, relevant websites that do not view themselves as shills for their company will prevail in the Google search as long as these companies follow good practices, continue to post even when they're too tired to do so, and look at their website as an extension of their company's marketing plan rather than a necessary evil.

CHAPTER 9:

Traditional Marketing Strategies You Should Never Neglect

Unless you're a company whose products, services and cus-tomers *only* interact on the web you'll have to spend some energy considering traditional marketing methods, such as promotions, trade shows and public relations. Some of you out there, I'll wager, spend a majority of your marketing dollars in these categories exclusively. There's a benefit in this that is usually not seen by marketers who only swim in the digital space. Fortunately, thanks to changing times, all three of these strategies have matured in recent years and offer much more than the uninitiated might be aware of.

Promotions Are No Longer Just Cheap Giveaways

Promotions are tricky to do well but valuable for businesses if you develop them properly. Although it is common practice for many companies to give incentives to their dealers with nothing more creative than bonuses on a sale, more strategic promotions find their footing in the development of two-tiered strategies (sometimes called vertical promotions) where companies provide motivations to buy for both the sales associates as well as the end users.

For several years I was a Creative Director of promotions for an agency whose clients were NBC Cable Networks, TNT, A&E, and Showtime, among others. Our job was to develop strategies to get affiliate stations (i.e., local broadcasters across the country that you would know better by their call letters, such as WOR or WKTU, than by their affiliation with particular networks) to run cross-channel promotions. In short, we were trying to run commercial spots that would entice viewers to change channels and go to the cable network of the client we represented.

To do this we found we had to make it worthwhile for affiliate program managers to get some kind of added value to their own jobs, lives, or community, and therefore increase their own positive PR. We also had to provide a promotional incentive for viewers to watch NBC's Olympic games on their associated cable station rather than on another outlet.

One of our more successful promotions created interest by offering the affiliates financing designated for goodwill projects in their local communities. The more cross-channel spots our affiliates ran, the more points they would receive toward a number of initiatives that would culminate in a money endowment to the charity of their choice or new books for school kids in the area. Being a vertical promotion, those points also benefitted the station manager with a "prize catalog" where he or she could trade in those points for an equal-value item, such as backpacks, toys, electronics, and the like.

Another series of successful promotions for A&E took advantage of the educational aspects of the shows it wanted to promote. For *St. Patrick*, *Les Misérables*, and *Horatio Hornblower*, our agency, Gem Group, produced classroom guides with projects that teachers could introduce as part of the curriculum. The finished projects would be part of a contest, and the winner would receive money for his or her school system. Consequently, nearly all the kids participating in these projects would inevitably watch those movies as part of the class assignment. As a result, A&E's ratings were attractive for all the programs we did this for.

These were just a few out-of-the-box promotional ideas that resonated with our clients. Although many B2B companies might not benefit from promotions that give away items consumers desire, it doesn't mean they can't get creative and increase their sales materials in the process. One way to do this is to give away your service or loan out your assets—for a price. For example, you send out a direct mailer or email blast offering 10 companies within your client base a product loaner, or free service, for a month if the client consents to appear in a testimonial video about its experience. At the end of the promotion, you'll have several testimonials and case studies that you can then, in turn, give to your sales force, post on YouTube, submit as press releases, and offer your potential clients a more compelling reason to buy into your company.

An Important Word About Promotional Incentives

Back in 2005, White Castle developed a promotion for one of its new products, the Roma Tomato Burger. Each store was outfitted with big banners, press releases were sent out, and an enormous effort was made to ensure this limited time meal was given its due.

While the Roma Tomato Burger was a moderate success, many of us who purchased it were surprised at what we got. Why? Because it was a regular White Castle hamburger with a slice of tomato on it. That's right. A slice of tomato, something you would get without asking at any other burger chain. Did White Castle really think the public would get excited and embrace the idea of a hamburger with a slice of tomato?

Even though the burgers themselves are remarkable and their *"What You Crave"* campaign is both on-target and hugely successful, their vision this time was slightly flawed (I say slightly because the burger did actually meet some numbers) in that the company tried to hype something that was unremarkable. What the company discovered, and should have known, was that most people are not that gullible.

To the same degree, promotions *need* to have a perceived value in their giveaways. To get potential customers to sign up and/or give you their information, the promotion must offer something in return that the customer wants. We've done a few promotions in the past where the customer was offered a free case study for filling in our submission form. On average, these promotions received little response unless aggressively promoted, which wasn't much of a surprise. If potential customers are willing to give up their contact information and possibly suffer through endless sales calls, the possibility of finding themselves on a marketing "list," and the disruption of their busy schedules, they sure as hell want something of more value in return.

There are two things I learned that resonated as well 10 years ago as they do today:

1. **Your incentive must have added value**

Customers are savvy. They know when they're being had. If you really want their contact information, you have to give them something that they, as buyers, are looking for. If you sell pool pallets to warehouses, maybe the offer of some free shrink-wrapping might fit the bill. If you are in the business of selling porcelain plates to restaurants, you might want to offer some free placemats to sweeten the deal. Most sales people deal in this type of bartering all day every day. The only difference with a promotion is you're making that offer up front. When there is added value to a customer's potential purchase, you "earn" that contact information.

2. **Your incentive should reinforce your brand**

Whatever it is you're offering, as in the examples above, it needs to complement your product or service and reinforce your brand. If you're a tool company, giving a pen away at a trade show is handy and might help a customer remember you when they're jotting down notes, but a branded Swiss Army knife might work better as a reminder of what it is you do. There are dozens of promotional incentive items to choose from, in addition to simply coming up with some unique ones on your own. For example, a CNN show on "Money & Power" that Vertical Mix was promoting included the promotional incentive (for affiliates) of the hardcover book version of the show, housed in a fancy cigar box. Reinforcement of the brand.

A much more cost-effective one for Great American Country's Summer BBQ promotion involved a branded oven mitt—once again, an item that resonated more with its intended audience than a simple branded flash drive or MP3 player would have.

Trade Shows Still Work... Depending on Your Market

There are two schools of thought about trade shows: they are a mandatory avenue to new clients or a complete waste of time. I think most of this perception gap has to do with companies that rely on such venues—and have had success, either directly or indirectly—and those whose business or demeanor are bad fits for these things. My company has several clients whose year relies on them. As a result, they direct a good portion of their marketing dollars toward booth graphics, promotions, upcoming campaigns (to entice their sales people and to let them know there will be large-scale "pushes" for particular products and services), and events within shows (dinners, awards) that keep their extended sales and distribution chains feeling wanted.

In tough times like these, companies that rely on shows are finding decreased traffic at such events. In this case, pre-show email lists are the most valuable commodity in reaching out to industry decision-makers and extending conversations through LinkedIn, email blasts, and other such connections.

For those who have not yet used trade shows as a venue for increased sales, it's certainly worth a shot, but be sure to spend your money on the shows that count. You're more than likely familiar with the most popular and well-attended shows in your business space. If not, this is something you should research thoroughly. There are many companies and organizations that produce shoddy, poorly attended shows that provide no bang for your buck. Sometimes, it's more cost effective to pay $200 and simply attend a show rather than pay $3,000, $10,000, or more to be an exhibitor at one. Many of the shows that ask for low-cost exhibit space can be a get-what-you-pay-for kind of endeavor. You might have better luck going from booth to booth, introducing yourself and making your connections that way.

The one great thing about interacting with trade show exhibitors (or attendees) is they are not immediately certain whether you are a benefit to them or not. As such, most people treat each other reasonably nice at these events, which means you might get an audience with a key decision-maker face-to-face that you might not through cold-calling or an email. You also could meet a potential vendor who leads you to a project, job, or distributor that you might not have had access to before. As you can see by simply doing a quick LinkedIn sweep, you're usually only a few people away from those you'd like to talk to anyway, so no type of networking is bad networking as long as you can capitalize on it in a useful way.

If you do decide to be an exhibitor, there are a few things you need to do to be competitive and look worthy, covered in the following sections.

Plan Your Event Early

There is nothing that wastes money more than being behind schedule on a trade show event. Furthermore, there are many marketing opportunities that will pass you by if you don't get on board early enough, from good ad positions in event directories and publications, to utilizing smart email blasts over several weeks that offer possible incentives toward products or services at your booth. In addition, online and offline advertising that will catch the eye of those in the industry who are pre-disposed to attending—with messaging that gives them your trade show booth number and even a name of who to speak to—will maximize your time at these events.

We also suggest you research the exhibitor and attendees lists. The most successful trade show attendees have done their due diligence before setting foot on the show floor. They know which companies they want to approach, who's in charge that they need to speak to and a little bit about their potential customers to show them they're sewn up, enthusiastic, and worth the time to talk to.

PR can also be a large part of your strategy here. If you can offer a preview of a new product or service and create excitement for it through a series of press releases (on the web or through the proper publications), you can be well on your way to making the show meaningful.

If your event takes place in a large hotel/convention center, there is a good likelihood that most of the attendees will be occupying rooms there. Printed materials that offer incentives, promotions, or sneak peeks can be slid under the hotel room doors a day prior or in the morning of the event. The key to all of this is planning. As a marketer, I've seen enormous opportunities wasted by clients who cannot get their act together in time for the shows that matter—and ALL OF THIS ties right back to your marketing plan. If you account for trade shows as part of your budget, you should also have a timetable ready to act on them.

Pay Attention to Floor Location

There's a psychology to choosing the right spot at a show. Some of it is common sense (don't be the last booth in the far corner of a convention center the size of a football field), but other times, a little bit of recon work takes the mystery out of where you should be. At industry events that are institutions, the best spots tend to go to the companies that have attended these shows regularly and have the most pull. Even those large companies that don't get the pick of the crop won't suffer too much. They are usually well known enough that traffic will find them based on their reputations or names. For smaller businesses, your best bet is to find a corner or island if you've got the material to justify it.

Design Your Booth to Make an Impact

Your booth doesn't have to put you in the poorhouse to make an impact, but it does need to make an impact. Like advertising, clever ideas and smart communication can put you on an even keel with the biggest players in your field. In addition, your message will always be more effective if it is consistent (once again, branding). Whatever message you adopt as the positioning statement of your company's marketing campaign should be mirrored at your trade show booth. Your trade show staff should also be briefed on this message and reinforce it whenever possible. Your collateral material and promotional elements should all be tied to the main message of your company. Look at it as a large magazine ad. Attendees are sometimes no different than potential customers perusing a magazine or browsing a website. Grab their attention by being clear, impactful, and eye-catching.

I also suggest renting a large-screen monitor and producing a company "loop." Graphic animation or video that can tell your company's story minus sound is a good way to inform attendees of who you are and what you do prior to contact with booth personnel. Once again, this all falls under the umbrella of making an impact in an environment where most companies simply "exist."

Move Around to Check out Your Competition

It's recommended that companies have at least two people at a show, not necessarily to do back-and-forth pitches to potential customers but so one person at all times can travel the show floor. This allows you to see what the competition is doing in addition to finding customers along the way and introducing yourself all over the place. Many are not comfortable with this kind of A-personality socializing, but trade shows are the one place where you can put your "game face" on and be that sales person you always thought you weren't. As I mentioned earlier, people are *interested* in talking to you (and trying their pitches out on you), so shyness is counterproductive here. Also, if you've planned well enough, you'll know your pitch (and have it whittled down to something quick and easy to grasp) and have the materials to back it up. There's nothing better than going into a room well-armed, knowing what your goal is and being prepared to meet it.

Prepare Follow-up Material

In addition to starting early, you will need to create materials that can be easily forwarded within days after the event, while your image and your company's image is still fresh in the minds of potential customers.

Public Relations: It's Not Just for Lady Gaga

Nearly all strategies associated with social marketing today are touted as if they are something new and unique. Start a blog! Write remarkable content! Get it published on more prominent online sites! Drive traffic back to your company!

All of these efforts have been the day-to-day of public relations since, well, forever. PR is invaluable, and to have a strong, viable advertising campaign, it is a necessary partner with traditional, online, and social marketing. Although you do need a great (and many times expensive) PR agency to get you known by the masses, many smaller ones in the B2B space are quite competent at getting your name, product, or service in front of the right customers at the right time.

PR, however, is busy work, which is one of the main reasons most PR agencies require a monthly retainer rather than a project-by-project budget. Good PR involves many people making many calls on your behalf, forging and/or utilizing relationships at trade publications and sites to place your story or press release (which they also write), and coordinating it with fresh or existing marketing campaigns. Where most social marketing books focus on links to content that exists on your site or blog (or are repurposed by blogs with back links to you) PR explores other avenues that'll ensure your company's message, products or presence are known.

Let's put it like this: An ad placement in a trade publication may cost you thousands, but an article will be worth 10 or 20 times that in the weight it will carry for customers. Buyers expect to see these products advertised and are blasé about the claims they find in them. It's a given that whatever they're reading in an ad is probably hype. On the other hand, an article that explores the benefits of a particular product is much more buzz-worthy—and when deciding between buzz and hype, most people will take the buzz, no questions asked. A "buzz" suggests others are impressed with your product or service. It's the equivalent of a great review on the most important blog in your industry. And enabling that review is part of the job description for most PR folks.

Our agency's marketing strategy nearly always involves a PR component, usually a press release sent out through PRWeb or ENewswire. Depending on the cost you agree on, these two services will make certain your article is published on high-ranking sites, guaranteeing a huge push for a website or promotion that otherwise would take weeks or months to be discovered across the web. Within a day of releasing your material on one or both of these two services, your article will be placed in the news section of Google, Newsday, USAToday. com, Yahoo News, Bing, ABCNews.com, AOL, CNBC and a whole host of others too numerous to name.

Rather than spending months trying to cultivate links through these or other prominent websites, many articles will become "sticky" on the sites above, including market-specific blogs within their network. Many times our agency has launched websites and promotions that, thanks to these submissions, moved clients quickly up the Google organic search, giving them solid positions in the first few pages that they managed to maintain for several months (and then continued to advance toward page one with subsequent press releases, white papers, and unique articles that got the message out). These articles always had their best days within the first week but still continued to find numerous placements several months later.

Pricing is anywhere from $89 per release to $369 (which gets your article published on premier sites such as New York Times, USA Today, Reuters and Associated Press).

Before and after important trade shows, our agency's PR department positions client articles in trades promoting these events; organizes dinners and conferences for clients; and is involved in the follow-up with potential clients, including Q&A sessions about the event and said client's needs. A good PR person (or strategy) is saltpeter to your marketing campaign or launch. They will make the most of the event and, if performed well, send leads your way in short order.

Types of Articles, News, and Releases

Much has been discussed about the type of articles, press releases, and essays that attract audiences best and become "sticky" across the web. There is no difference here for B2B clients. The material you use to promote yourself needs to be, first and foremost, entertaining and informative. Anything short of that is a lost cause.

Seth Godin talks about creating "remarkable content" as a way to entice viewers to take notice of you and spread your message. I can't agree more. However, the gap between creating content and creating remarkable content is huge. Nonetheless, there are some tried-and-true methods to creating content that others will want to read and bloggers will want to include on their own sites:

1. **The list**

Lists are seductive. Good ones become viral. They are a great way for businesses to market in two primary ways: First, they give your customers (or potential customers) snippets of advice that are easy to digest and valuable. Second, they show that you (the giver of advice) have knowledge that they can use and haven't considered before, or simply show that you are sewn up in your thinking. As an expert, you can take complex or complicated issues and break them down into easy-to-understand jargon. It will also show that you are organized enough in your thinking to know HOW to dissect a problem. For example, if you are an Internet security company, you might consider writing an article entitled "10 Ways to Ensure Your Computer Security" or "5 Computer Viruses and How to Avoid Them." Great lists can account for hundreds if not thousands of links and potential customers; even mediocre lists will generate interest in bloggers, given the hunger for content and an appealing format that never ceases to attract the curious.

2. **The question**

Questions are provocative. Everyone wants to know the answer to a good question. Questions guarantee that your audience will read further and these articles are easy for you, the expert, because you usually know that answer before asking it. If you are a law firm that specializes in corporate litigation, an article entitled "Are You Certain Your Company Is Not Under Investigation?" could elicit a huge interested audience. What you do with a question-posed article is offer your customers the advice they have made the effort to seek out (either through the web or a trade magazine), and an answer that makes you the expert they didn't know they were also searching for.

3. The instruction

As I mentioned in Chapter 1, I am a big fan of the Dyson vacuum cleaner commercials. They are instructive, simple, and elegant. They explain what is unique about their product and the thinking behind it. In 30 seconds, they do what most companies have tried and failed to do in 30 years. Instructional content varies. For some customers, like the dealers and integrators for Canon's broadcast lenses, details such as specifications and unique features, and how they are used, are hugely important. For other customers, cost, profit, and support are the primary focus. Whatever end of the spectrum your clients fit, it's best to be entertaining as well as informative, break up your text through numbering (as this section of this chapter does) or use catchy headlines for different paragraphs that break down the discussion.

4. The Q&A

Audiences are brought up on interviews. They encounter them on the news, entertainment programs, and talk shows. They are also easy to browse through, and readers can take away as little or as much of it that they want. With a ready audience that is predisposed to finding Q&A sessions inviting, an interview with a company executive about a product or service (or, for that matter, using a client testimonial) is invaluable. It gives the customer the ability to casually absorb vital information about your product or service without feeling that it's being spoon-fed.

5. Case studies and white papers

For business customers, a case study and white paper can make the difference between whether your product makes it to the next level of approval or not. Middle managers do not always have the time to become experts on every purchase they make. As a result, expert testimony from previous clients may be all the ammunition they need to show they've done their due diligence and can pass the process along to the next in line. It also puts you a step above your competition, particularly if that competition either doesn't have case studies or white papers, or has not made them available in an easy way to mass media.

Smart content, and a variety of it, will win you links across the web. This kind of social marketing isn't useful for every business, but for those that it is, you can't go wrong being entertaining, informative, and helpful.

Sponsorships and Affiliations

For companies who find the right opportunity or have enough cash in their budgets to justify the expense, sponsoring events is a great way to get your company's name out there. In keeping with smart branding techniques, it is always best to sponsor events that have some relevance to your product or service. For example, Nike has probably sponsored more runs and walks than can be accurately counted. The company will continue to do countless more, because its product blends perfectly into the purpose of the event. Also, the audience for such events, particularly sports on TV, can lend itself to unusual bedfellows. For example, thanks to the creative thinking of one of my long-time clients, Hass Avocados from Mexico spent several years as the sponsor of the sports car driven by Dave Blaney (no relation). Known in racing circles as the "Hass Car," Blaney's impressive record and name recognition helped the company's logo stay front and center for the NASCAR audience, part of which were the wives of NASCAR fans. When those same wives went to the grocery store the next day, they would see that same logo again on display in the produce section, with an image of the Hass Car right next to it. This campaign succeeded thanks to repetition and the shrewd strategy of knowing where the core audience was.

Whereas some B2B clients can obviously afford such sponsorship gold (take a look at Citi Field in NY as a perfect example), smaller companies might find themselves left out of the big picture. Nonetheless, sponsorships can be found at local events, and it just takes a little research to find the type of event that could suit your company well.

For companies with less funding, affiliate marketing is another worthy avenue. Essentially, you become part of several "partners" in a promotion or event. An affiliate marketer will usually suggest an existing or upcoming event that you could benefit from by having your service or product offered free, in exchange for your name being prominently displayed in ads. Another option is to develop a promotion from scratch that benefits all affiliates involve. For example, in the past I helped develop "getaway" promotions where the lucky winner would get a free vacation (courtesy of an affiliate hotel chain), free airfare (courtesy of an affiliate airline), and an assortment of gifts (courtesy of a couture of appropriately chosen companies with products and services that complemented the theme of the getaway).

Like advertising, these events and promotions coax partici-
pators to find out more about your company. By using mobile
barcodes or merchandise giveaways, you can help to continue
the conversation—and the sale—to your website, microsite, or
mobile app.

The Re-Emergence of Business Video

I began my career producing industrial videos back in the late
'80s. Most of them were for pharmaceutical outfits (such as
Pfizer, Bristol-Meyer Squibb and others), and the budgets were
pretty outlandish. Then again, they had to be: the equipment was
expensive (back then, a standard Ikegami camcorder cost
around $20,000 to $50,000 in today's money); the crews and
directors were equally expensive; and editing required booking
expensive studios where every feature was a la carte. Animation
and 3D artwork? Hell, only the big guys had that. We were
stuck debating on whether to use a wipe or a dissolve as our
only graphic effects. Inevitably, most videos looked professional but were hardly noteworthy, and production and distribution of these videos remained out of reach for most mid-sized
companies.

Today, however, good, professional, slick video productions are within reach of every company (and, for that matter,
every individual). What's more, with the majority of customers
in the United States tapped into high-speed Internet service,
streaming, high-definition digital productions are the norm.
Aesthetics have also become more varied. Courtesy of image-
stabilization software, smooth hand-held shots are no longer
the domain of great, gymnastic professional camera people but
can be produced with relative ease by a two-year-old.

And editing? Well, buying editing software today is as easy
as purchasing versions of Microsoft Word. If you have enough

hard drive space, you can create your own office editing studio just as easily.

What all this means is that the typical video production no longer costs an arm and a leg. As a result, companies can spend when they want to spend (for truly slick, TV-network-quality productions) and go smaller when they want volume. In today's business landscape, video has become the new telephone call. Why work your pitch over the phone or fly to Arizona when you can just as easily tell your lead to watch a video case study and then follow up later?

Now, most hardcore sales people might chafe at that as a new business strategy, and I wouldn't blame them. There will always need to be a boots-on-the-ground approach, but whether video is used as one of many marketing tools at a salesperson's disposal or as the primary tool in making a potential customer comfortable with a sale, it will, from this point forward, be a player.

The immediacy of this medium gives companies the opportunity to add visuals to what, in the past, were press releases, case studies, and white papers. Furthermore, the vastness of the web also allows companies to introduce audiences and direct potential customers to media that used to be available only to qualified leads after a successful sales call. Let's look at a few different types of video.

Customer Testimonial Videos

Word of mouth doesn't have to grow organically. It doesn't need to be out of a company's control. When a product or service does take off and referrals are the main source of new business, it's always the most welcome of events, but your marketing plan need not wait for that to happen before making your case.

Testimonial videos for business fit the bill for business

clients. These videos are not sexy or clever or imaginative or colorful, but they do provide the most important ingredient: direct word of mouth. And they're stories told directly to potential customers, by others just like those customers. Never underestimate the power of looking into the eyes of another human being. All the sexy products shots in the world will never have the caché of a strongly worded recommendation, straight from the horse's mouth.

Also, if there is more than one individual involved in using your product or service, you can then interview several people from the same company. One of our most effective videos involved a plant in Arkansas where my client's product had replaced more antiquated equipment that had been around for years. By intercutting between four people, all of whom worked in different parts of the plant's workforce, the video built a compelling narrative about the client's products that was surprisingly cohesive, clear, and organized into three parts: a discussion of the company's needs, how the decision was made to go with my client's product, and how my client's product improved productivity at this customer's plant.

Before embarking on this type of video, it's wise to define what you hope to be the narrative of these interviews. That will help to define the questions you ask your subjects off-camera. You'll be surprised at how verbose most clients get when a camera lens is pointed at them, and how instinctive it is for them to frame your product or service in a complimentary way. But usually, it's enough to have them tell the story in their own voice.

Product or Service Videos
What is better than to have a captive audience as you explain to all how your product or service works? That's one of the benefits of a product or service video.

Truth be told, these types of videos are rarely the go-to content for viewers casually perusing the web, but are just fine for B2B purposes. If you position your video properly, apply correct keywording and use your social channels well, you will find the audience you need.

Product and service videos are great in two ways. First, they provide a needed respite for potential customers who would rather absorb information than research it. Your video takes the "work" out of their task of reading through articles, comparing features, and blindly assessing whether you or your company are reliable or trustworthy. Second, it gives you the opportunity to be several places at once by performing as a standalone sales tool for customers in different states (or, for that matter, countries). Product and service videos also allow you to make the case as to how and why your product or service works better than your competitors'. You can offer a discount for potential customers to mull over, or a link to a lead-generation tool.

How-to Videos

Most of us search the web to learn; the internet was a research tool long before it was a source of entertainment. Considering that, it's not surprising that how-to videos are very popular. For any company, it's always a good approach to display your level of expertise for others to see and how your "process" works better than the rest. It's understandable that some of you will feel the need to keep company secrets secret; however, although some secrets deserve that consideration (like the KFC chicken recipe, for example), most will not embolden your competition to launch a strategy to destroy you. In most cases, how-to videos turn regular folks like you into experts. As an expert, you are likely to find more business opportunities than you'll need. No downside there.

The other benefit of this medium is it is naturally built

to be modular. Your videos could be part of a series that bring in more viewers. Having produced how-to series before, I've found that success usually comes from one video over all others on the web. It also gives you great insight into what your audience values most in the answers to the questions you pose, and that can help engage them in future videos.

Webinars

I've read that webinars can be described as a breakout session of a trade-show booth, and I think that's the best way to characterize it. Webinars, short for "web-based seminars," are presentations, lectures, or workshops transmitted over the web. They usually happen live, but some have been recorded and offered after the fact. For the right B2B company, a webinar is a way to have a captive audience to make your sales pitch to, and have all the material on hand to illustrate what's great about your product or service. There are several things to consider when producing a webinar, such as:

1. **Invite enough people**

   The key to a successful webinar is making sure you have a good list of prospective clients in mind. Like a party where no one shows up, nothing is worse than hosting a webinar and having only a handful of people make an appearance (unless they are the key decision makers you've dreamed of).

2. **Choose a good speaker**

   It's important to make certain your speaker (if it is not going to be you) is engaging and entertaining. Nobody wants to sit through a boring lecture, particularly when they have a full plate of work to dig through, as your audience most likely will.

3. Make the PowerPoint engaging

A great PowerPoint is a mixture of pleasing graphics, streamlined ideas, and visual surprises. It doesn't have to have fancy animation flying through it to work, but it should complement the speaker rather than call attention to all the speaker is not discussing. Spare is better.

4. Keep it short

30 minutes is a substantial amount of time. Anything more, and you'll see your audience begin to drop out of sight.

5. Offer an incentive for showing up

Your listeners are investing their time rather than doing something else (or reading the competitor's website). They deserve an incentive for that. A white paper that is not available online could be an option, or you might offer a percentage off on the client's first sale.

6. Don't be "the sales guy"

Your audience is there to be informed and enlightened. It is not there for an aggressive sales pitch. How many times have you received an email claiming you've won a prize, only to call up and find out it's nothing of the sort? Respect those who show up by giving them something substantial to leave the webinar with.

7. Make it a Q&A

Most B2B webinars involve a speaker dictating material to his or her audience. If your audience is small enough (fewer than 25 people), you may have the opportunity to take a few questions and turn your event into something a little more intimate.

8. **Follow it up**

This should be the golden rule for every sales person in every company everywhere. *Always* follow up with your leads. I've seen many good leads that our agency has sent to our clients go nowhere, simply because there wasn't the manpower (or womanpower) to get back to people who have displayed interest in their product. A webinar is a perfect example of an event where your audience is clearly sold in. A thank-you email is always in order, and the fruit of your labor could be close at hand—a sale.

CHAPTER 10:

What Do We Do with the Leads?

Your marketing plan is implemented. You've built your branding campaign, updated your website, hit all the appropriate social markets, and have lead generation activities that are ongoing. You're finally beginning to see the fruits of your labor as potential customers respond to your calls-to-action and discover your videos, press releases, blog postings, print and web campaigns. Now what?

As mentioned before, many of these leads go nowhere. Why? Because no one pursues them. They slip through the cracks and become unanswered emails and phone calls. If your company truly wants to make a return on investment with your marketing it is crucial that you make lead nurturing a must for your sales people.

Lead nurturing must be institutional

At any reasonably sized B2B company you'll find one constant—the diametrically opposed viewpoints of both the sales and marketing departments about how to find and manage leads best.

Even though I'm a marketing guy, I understand the sales team's frustration; many of them receive leads through efforts that are uneven, weak, or sometimes based on faulty customer profiles. They embrace them initially and, when they don't turn up as quick sales, they dismiss all of them outright thereafter. Marketing teams, on the other hand, can receive vague directives from sales that, in turn, affect their planning and strategy. As a result, valuable insight into the psychology and buying habits of a sales target are never fully integrated into the marketing materials.

Solution? Marketing: Bring the sales team in earlier. Sales: Provide the kind of input marketing needs to get you your qualified leads. Afterward, both departments need to work together, create customer profiles together (and sign off on them) have monthly meetings, and be clear on why certain leads are not bearing fruit. It's not a competition. It shouldn't be a rivalry. It's all about lead conversion—and putting more money into everyone's pockets, whether it's through salary or commission.

Types of Leads

When a potential customer appears, you need first to define what kind of lead you have and put a process in place to respond to them. Whether you have a sales team or sales person, they will very likely try to break them out into one of the following categories:

Soft Leads

"I'm considering your type of service. Please provide more details."
For some businesses, this kind of response, followed by an email address (but maybe not a phone number) is akin to what we'd call a "soft lead." These kind of leads follow a call-to-action that involves very little risk for the potential customer, or may show up as a result of a promotional or sweepstakes campaign. They are by nature vague, and the lack of detail can be either the M.O. of someone of few words, or a hard lead in disguise.

Hard Lead

"I'm interested in purchasing twenty new solar panels for our campus. Please give me a call."
These leads may come through your funnel less frequently, but, as you know, they are the ones that appear with a big, red flashing light. Hard leads could follow a form attached to a downloadable case study, a long form available on your website, or a phone number at the end of a 10-minute video on your product. What's most important is a quick follow-up.

Referrals

"I got your name from a colleague of mine. He claims you're the best in the business at what you offer..."
Referrals are not only word-of-mouth. They can be the result of a conversation in a chat room or forum where others discuss your business service, the phone number available below a testimonial video from a satisfied client of yours, or participation in a professional organization through your own relationship with those who run them. Without question, referrals are the most ideal of leads. They come to businesses already vetted. What businesses do with them at that point is up to them.

After qualifying these leads, your sales team has to have a strategy for following through. There are some tried and true methods for nurturing leads at this point and, sometimes, the nature of your prospect will tell you much of what you need to know about how to approach them:

Respond to them quickly

According to a lead response management study presented by InsideSales.com, leads that become qualified are done so mostly within the first five minutes after the request is made and the sales person makes the contact. Every five minutes afterward decreases the chance of qualifying that lead. We live in a fast-paced environment where customers expect answers immediately. While some B2B customers take longer to determine who their vendors will be for products and services, responding quickly to their inquiries is mandatory whether they are feeling you out or ready to pull the trigger on a purchase.

Know what you're talking about

Nobody wants to listen to someone who has a boilerplate speech or a vague understanding of the products or services they're selling. The best way to win over a potential customer is to let him or her know that you know what you're talking about. Companies with in-house sales departments should ensure these teams are up to date with current products, literature, features and services—and understand them well enough to give them more than just lip service.

Sometimes internal promotions give salespeople and company representatives a greater incentive to learn what they need to know. One of our most successful internal promotions at Chase Small Business involved three multiple-choice "tests" that salespeople were persuaded to answer. If they did, they were given the opportunity of winning 10,000 frequent flyer miles or one of three second-tier prizes. The promotion was placed on their intranet and those who participated were added to a company list available for view on one of the promotion pages. We made it fun and it not only resulted in having sales teams across the country better educated on new Chase products, but due to the visibility of the participants, the program had an 88% participation rate.

Get them to go to second base with you

We all remember the Seinfeld episode where George implements his dating strategy of leaving behind a personal item at a date's apartment. His theory is that if he can get them to accept a second date with him—even if it is just to return the item—he's got a better chance of future dates. While most salespeople are a world more confident than George Costanza, there should be a multi-tiered strategy for getting a potential customer to take the next step and confirming that opportunity to speak again. As long as it's about a legitimate sales goal, it'll make you more than just another sales call. It makes you a familiar voice and provides the beginnings of a "relationship."

Keep them in the loop

When the sales lead is targeted but unwilling to make a purchase, don't just throw that lead away unless you're certain it's an absolute dud. While they may not be your customer in this sales cycle, they could very well be one in the future. Include them in product and service updates through email blasts and always offer no-charge advice or help when they need it. The best sales people I know are nothing if not persistent and nurture some leads for years until they pay off.

For customers who find your company through the web, keeping them in the loop includes newsletters, social marketing updates, business-based publications created by you or your company, and any incentives or promotions that could sweeten a potential deal.

There are also other products for furthering your reach to potential customers and, like getting all the meat out of a steamed lobster, you could see potential business where in places you've not searched prior. Knowing how to use these tools is half the battle.

Tracking Leads and Traffic: Tracking Software

There are many different forms of tracking software out there, and most of them works well for those who use them. A good many of the online properties our agency has created combine the following tracking products:

1. *Webtrends*
2. *Clicky*
3. *Sitemeter*
4. *Google Analytics*
5. *Extreme-DM*
6. *Awstats*

While Webtrends is the gold standard for those who want detailed reports on tracking and customer behavior, less expensive software can sometimes give you extended tracking variables that fit the bill just fine for your company. Sitemeter, in my mind, is one of the best types of software for the money (which is as little as $14.94 a month for up to 100,000 page views). Unlike Google Analytics and some of the others, Sitemeter shows you the referring URL page and the out click. It tracks the exact amount of time each viewer stays on your website and the amount of pages that viewer viewed. What it doesn't show you is every single page that viewer has seen. To accommodate that analysis, we also use the Pro Tracker from Extreme-DM.

Sitemeter generates code based on your web URL. You simply place it between the <body> tags on your website, or in the footer of a modular site. After a day or two, you will be able to make some judgments on who's coming to your website and how they are finding you. For our clients, we are also able to siphon off leads from time to time from users who don't necessarily leave their contact information in our contact page. The way we do this is as follows:

Our first step is to peruse the "By Details" view of recent visitors. Sitemeter provides you with the IP address (or provider) the time at which they visited, their page views, and the length of time they stayed on. If you click on one of the numbers next to the IP address, you will find a screen that looks like the image below:

recent visitors	
By Details	
By Referrals	
By World Map	
By Location	
By Out Clicks	
By Entry Pages	
By Exit Pages	
visits	
Current Day	
Previous 7 Days	
Previous 30 Days	
Previous 12 Months	
visits and page views	
Current Day	
Previous 7 Days	
Previous 30 Days	
Previous 12 Months	
page ranking	
Entry Pages	
Exit Pages	
support+service	
KnowledgeCenter	
Submit Support Request	
Upgrade Account	

Domain Name	(Unknown)	
IP Address	192.54.250.# (Pratt & Whitney)	
ISP	Pratt & Whitney	
Location	Continent : North America	
	Country : United States (Facts)	
	State : California	
	City : Reseda	
	Lat/Long : 34.2005, -118.5404 (Map)	
Language	English (U.S.) en-us	
Operating System	Microsoft WinXP	
Browser	Internet Explorer 7.0 Mozilla/4.0 (compatible; MSIE 7.0; Windows NT 5.1; .NET CLR 1.1.4322; .NET CLR 2.0.50727; InfoPath.1)	
Javascript	version 1.3	
Monitor	Resolution : 1280 x 1024 Color Depth : 32 bits	
Time of Visit	Nov 7 2011 3:21:19 pm	
Last Page View	Nov 7 2011 3:21:45 pm	
Visit Length	26 seconds	
Page Views	1	
Referring URL	http://www.google.co...rtIndex=&startPage=1	
Search Engine	google.com	
Search Words	hospital boilers	
Visit Entry Page	http://www.steamboilersforhospitals.com/	
Visit Exit Page	http://www.steamboilersforhospitals.com/	

This screen provides you a full accounting of the visitor. Sometimes you'll see the viewer's name, depending on the type of hosting account the viewer has. You may also discover how these individuals stumbled onto your website (in this case, a search for "hospital boilers" on Google where we come up as position number one), and the actual time the viewer was online. If you want more details of each person's visit that might not be available in Sitemeter, you can download the raw data log from your website control panel. Matching the IP address with the visitor in question, you'll find a full accounting of every section of your website that person viewed, in addition to any functions the viewer used or attempted to use (such as contact page submission forms). Before long, you have a pretty solid profile of your visitor and whether there might be some client potential there.

What I tend to do first when pursuing a lead is check the Sitemeter page on referring sites. As you can see in the image below, you may also find references to your website in places you were previously unfamiliar with. In this case, we tracked the link for "Firecad.net" and found a forum on boilers. Clicking on this link, we discovered a potential client whose post on a forum alludes to a need for our client's product:

A few quick searches in Google combining the IP address and an .edu listing, and it's pretty easy to find your potential lead. Some of these searches turn up as dead ends, others as client potential. The trick is knowing what you're looking for.

On the back end of your website, your free Awstats software gives a quick accounting of what your website's day looks like so far. This is the default tracking software used on most Unix-based hosts. Although it's best to not make much of the "hits" (because they refer to nearly every element that exists on each page seen, and therefore, 20 hits could very likely be one page view), you can track individual surfers by matching their IP numbers from those found through Sitemeter and ExtremeDM.

Customer Relationship Management (CRM)

If you are a large manufacturer with dealers around the country who rely on your customer support to help them seal the deal, you might want to consider the help of a CRM. These systems, which can be fully automated or supplemented with actual human support, help large companies filter leads, build lead databases, nurture existing customers through outreach, and manage every part of the sales process. They also track a campaign's effectiveness through social, email, and SEO advertising.

While CRMs can include call centers, appointment setters and direct phone-based customer service, recent trends show companies are moving toward cloud-based software that can be monitored through web browsers.

The biggest challenge with tapping into the potential of these programs is, once again, the adoption of it by salespeople and company officials alike. For salesmen, many CRMs provide a place for updates on leads. They are expected to amend captured information with an on-the-ground account of a sales call or sales visit. Helpful for the company? Sure. Productive for the salesperson? Well, that may be debatable on their end. For many, this software is extra work at the end of the day. If you can find, or modify, a CRM that allows your sales people to make updates quickly on the phone—either through a voice file or a flew clicks of a button as they drive from one lead to the next—you may have more converts to these systems than some companies currently do.

Don't drop the ball

Whether you decide on managing leads internally, personally, or through a CRM, the ROI for your marketing can only be measured correctly when all avenues of sale have been exhausted. Just remember: these marketing efforts combined represent a hardworking new business person who understands your company well, knows all the correct places to look for customers, and keeps at it daily, weekly, monthly. When legitimate leads surface through this employee's efforts, consider them valid, follow up, and reap the benefit.

CHAPTER 11:

B2B Success Stories

What good would a book about B2B be without actual success stories? This chapter describes a few companies that have tried something new and how they've fared.

CerviLenz:
Even a Medical Equipment Manufacturer
Can Have a Social Network

BKV, a Kansas City digital and direct marketing agency, had been handling traditional marketing for CerviLenz (a manufacturing company that sold a device used by obstetricians, labor and delivery at hospitals, and nurses/midwives) when it decided to explore the idea of reaching that audience through the social space.

After researching their customers on the web, BKV discovered that a substantial number of nurses/midwives were using Facebook to connect and talk. As is the makeup of any well-researched marketing campaign, BKV and CerviLenz's strategy was multi-pronged. Their goal was to:

- *Target audience awareness*
- *Increase visits to the company website*
- *Build a sustainable audience online that could be seeded with extra product information*
- *...and find a way to get visitors to their trade show booths*

What they did was create a Facebook page that catered to the nurse/midwife audience, while also addressing needs of their other customers. During the buildout of their Facebook channel, they were also able to draw potential customers to their booth through incentives and promotions. They also created a "Give Back" promotion that served as a donation channel for prevention of premature deliveries, a particularly smart and charitable strategy that any B2B customer can justify getting involved in.

As a result of these efforts, CerviLenz now has more than 1,800 fans on its Like page and 10% of referral traffic, including more than 5,000 visits to its About tab. It's a perfect example of how the proper research, and a bit of micromarketing, can find customers in places never before mined through B2B channels.

UPS – The New Logistics

In Chapter 2, I mentioned UPS's Whiteboard commercials,

which were shown exclusively in the United States. Another campaign, UPS's 2010 "We Love Logistics" (developed through Ogilvy & Mather), was UPS's first global endeavor. The huge budget for this initiative didn't skimp on old media, but the surprise here was its use of new tools: this campaign was one of the first to strongly leverage UPS's social networking acumen. It did so by creating a series of online marketing tools that interconnect and answer nearly every question customers could possibly have (the customers, in this case, being small businesses).

UPS did this first by creating a website, TheNewLogistics.com, which drew heavily on case studies and was also destination where customers could find:

- *Many examples of small business successes from using UPS shipping*
- *Clever tools that calculate the savings you can achieve by using UPS*
- *Explanations of the scale and scope of UPS (in as much detail as you can handle)*
- *Videos that explain the various philosophies on how UPS helps its customers*
- *A blog called Upside, which offers up more recent case studies, tips, and ideas*

As a result of this effective marketing, the campaign cultivated leads through:

- *A Facebook page that earned over 28,000 fans*
- *A Twitter account with 7,436 followers*
- *A YouTube page that has averaged over 8,000 views for its numerous videos*

ShipServ

Maritime is the last industry you'd expect to have a robust social media strategy, but ShipServ is an exception. ShipServ is an e-marketplace solution for ship owners, managers, yards, and drilling contractors; the company creates software that links buyers to products and suppliers around the world. Its proprietary tool, TradeNet, has more than 5,000 ships, 150 shipping companies, and more than 30,000 suppliers registered to it. ShipServ conducted an e-commerce survey (in April 2010, Watton 2010) and found that a majority of its customers consider social media in the shipping business to be a "distracting waste of time." Given that reaction, how could ShipServ create a successful B2B campaign that encourages its customers to interact online?

The company's first and boldest step was believing it was possible. Its research also unveiled an important detail: the company's target customers were very interested in networking any way they could, but they saw themselves as a "paper-and-phone"-based community. As a result, ShipServ felt the best way to engage its target customers was first to discover where they congregated on the web. Using their Google Adwords account, ShipServ was able to identify the most common and oft-used terms for discussion in its industry and, through web aggregator Netvibes, it managed to track down conversations about the industry as well as ShipServ itself.

After discovering that ShipServ was rarely named in conversations with potential customers, the company set forth to change that dynamic. The first step was a revamp of the company website. ShipServ.com went from being a large corporate brochure (which is the bane of most B2B companies) to becoming something much more useful: an industry hub for customers. The next thing the company did was "talk up" its current customers through its case studies. The company also developed a blog, but it did so with a firm strategy in mind. Its content would be developed around six themes of varied media: white papers, blog posts, tweets, e-newsletters, viral videos, and podcasts. The company fine-tuned its LinkedIn and Facebook accounts to take as much advantage of new posts as possible within its control. In addition, the company utilized PitchEngine.com, a rich-media news release website, to get its message out. The benefit of PitchEngine is three fold: It ranks high on search engines, it's easy to use, and it allows customers to do more than just post a press release (you can include video and imagery that are easy for news organizations to repurpose).

Finally, throughout all this new content, ShipServ veered away from the standard corporate speak and decided to have more fun with its audience. Viral videos with humor became a quick avenue to the new website. Remarkable content written in "humanspeak" found audiences beyond maritime industry circles, which also helped push ShipServ up on the organic search. The company's e-newsletter was used as an opinion piece and promotion vessel: for example, ShipServ's contest to "name the newsletter" received 200 responses and increased its newsletter customer base in the process. Free case studies were offered through all media channels. And this entire process was continued month after month.

The company's efforts paid off. A new LinkedIn group, "ShipServ Maritime Trading Network," was developed and promoted as a community that would bring together companies and suppliers. As a result of its research, the company was also able to join five existing communities in their space; ShipServ provided content and conversation to these groups but also returned the favor. As a result of listening well, ShipServ was able to blog about subjects it knew were important to the community. In short order, ShipServ became a thought leader, had 863 members in its LinkedIn group, and its return on investment was achieved within three months (courtesy Haakon Jenson) :

- *Website statistics (First quarter of 2009):*
  - *Visitors increased by 59%*
  - *Pageviews increased by 70%*
  - *Average time on site increased by 25%*
  - *Generated more than 1,000 downloads of a white paper*
- *Community statistics:*
  - *378 in the Maritime Network group on LinkedIn*
  - *300 visitors to the blog*
  - *More than 50 relevant followers on Twitter*
  - *More than 600 views of the viral videos (62% through email distribution and 18% through Shipserv.com/LinkedIn)*
  - *LinkedIn and Twitter from zero to top 20 traffic sources*
- *Business statistics:*
  - *Increased contact-to-lead conversion by 150%*
  - *Increased lead-to-opportunity conversion by 50%*
  - *Decreased campaign management costs by 80%*
  - *Increased the number of sales-ready leads by 400%*

HD Camera Guide

HD Camera Guide's success was hardly by accident. Prior to releasing it, our agency had already developed another "guide" for health care: *HealthSiteGuide.com*. Much of what we learned in HSG would later be used to promote and subsequently build HDCG.

In 2007, we developed HD Camera Lens Guide. Its purpose was to promote high-end line of HD lenses, which were used primarily on Broadcast and ENG (Electronic News

Gathering) cameras. At the time we developed this site, our client's division sold and serviced professional lenses for professional users. These clients were TV stations, large sports venues, electronic news gatherers, and motion picture houses, among many others. Unlike electronic consumer products, which competed with many brands on the market, broadcast lenses were narrowly focused. The goal was to be the primary addition to expensive cameras made by Ikegami, JVC, Sony, Panasonic, and other companies. Our client's main competition were other lens manufacturers.

Our audience was very specific. These lenses have never been, and will never be, consumer items, so the target was the professional user base and those who buy camera equipment for them. The fact of the matter is that most cameramen cannot afford lenses that ranged in price from $25,000 to $200,000, so our target audience were AV buyers at large-media outlets— places like ESPN or a large television studio and, in particular, the people in charge whose job it is to buy these products for their companies.

Initially, HD Camera Lens Guide was a Flash-based application that displayed lens options that corresponded with three drill-down categories: camera manufacturer, type of camera (for example, portable or box), and a particular model name. While we were developing the guide, we pondered expansion of the idea to include information about the camera manufacturer and its products. At the time, there was no existing website that we could find that catered purely to the broadcast buyer, and the existing trade publication mainstays (i.e., Broadcast Engineering, Sound And Video, and TV Technology) were not pure niches, because their online counterparts were merely duplicates of their printed material. We felt that we could attract the audience by creating more videos, providing more information about particular cameras (without a bias that would usually be found from a dealer or wholesaler), and try to be a "partner" with the audience that made these purchases. In short, our ability to connect with our audience let them know that we weren't taking sides, and we could start a real conversation that provided information, advice, and feedback.

As for platform, we chose Joomla as our application. As mentioned in Chapter 5, Joomla has proven to be a search engine magnet, with a flexible enough structure to fit our vision.

IBM – Innov8 and CityOne

IBM's WebSphere is a software application server that was first launched by Big Blue in 1998. The software is best known as "middleware"; in layman's terms, it is software applications used by end users to integrate their existing business applications with others. A kind of digital glue, you might say.

In 2009, IBM's marketers decided to try a different strategy to increase sales and drive interest in its product by using a promotional gimmick previously attributed to the consumer side: a game. Knowing they needed to educate their audience on what is a very complex series of products (even for software engineers), they felt the best approach might be to entertainingly "guide" them through the features as if they were at home playing a corporate version of Grand Theft Auto.

Innov8 demo users are quickly immersed in a CGI world where a company needs to find ways to improve its traffic, call centers, and supply chains. They are given puzzles to solve, first-person environments to navigate through, and questions to answer from the company executives that all lead to a win. According to Sandy Carter, Vice President of IBM Software Group Business Partners, "We're not just using gaming for education, although we are doing that. But we're actually using gaming to generate leads and create community." And a community is exactly what was created around this unique marketing tool. The greatest benefit of IBM doing something so drastically different within its marketing approach was, according to Carter, how well the "experience sticks with them."

IBM spread the word about the demo through its existing social network of hundreds of employee bloggers and their followers. Also, having been a large user of crowd-sourcing in the communication channels with developers and users, IBM gained a reputation as a company that builds products based on actually "listening" to its customers instead of dictating. As a result, Innov8 has become the company's number one lead-generation tool for the WebSphere brand.

Following its success with Innov8, IBM launched its City-One game in 2010 at its Impact Conference to educate the public on business and environmental problems that plague every city and, not surprisingly, how some of these solutions might involve the use of IBM software. Nancy Pearson, another IBM vice president, suggests that this type of out-of-the-box marketing solutions give customers a much clearer picture of how the power of IBM software can be used to solve their own business challenges in a way "hazy brand campaigns" can't. It's another great example of how innovation, both in a company's product or service as well as its marketing, can change the game and find new customers, without simply relying on the old standbys.

Idea Paint

A startup from Ashland, Massachusetts is one of the best examples of how a company culture that embraces social media can power success in marketing. Idea Paint sells a unique single coat paint product that turns every wall surface into a dry-eraser board. It's a product that has been marketed to schools (to replace chalkboards) and businesses (to replace clumsy paper pads).

Idea Paint created a blog, but it wasn't the act of creating the blog that generated leads. It was what the company populated it with and how the company spread the word beyond the blog to get customers to take notice. The blog has been, primarily, a host to a number of case studies. Many have been committed to video (and pushed through the company's own optimized YouTube channel). Idea Paint also encouraged customers to provide their own photos of how they've used the product, and Idea Paint has integrated those elements into its marketing push.

The company also spread the word through Facebook. Idea Paint has amassed more than 5,000 followers on a very active Twitter page—and it actively seeks out potential customers talking about its product with whom they can interact. They've created an enormous and robust Flickr channel for all their videos as well as customer photos (which the company categorizes for easy search) that have received thousands of views and include hundreds of search tags. Idea Paint is also an early adopter of Pinterest, which duplicates most of its customer photos. The company has also developed promotions, such as its *IdeaPaint360 Makeover Contest*, which have helped to increase potential customers on all its social channels (as promotions will always do). Idea Paint has utilized Hubspot for its keyword grader and consulting services, to increase awareness of the company across the web. As a result of its efforts, Idea Paint grew 70% in the first quarter of 2010 and has risen significantly since then.

CHAPTER 12:

If Not Now, When?

I began writing this book a year before I published it. Why? Because I'm an idiot. Sure, it's an accomplishment to get anything done when you are busy doing the work of three people, have family obligations and countless other expectations heaped on you, but a year is too long in today's terms.

Just like my writing here should have been available six months earlier than it was, changing the course of your marketing cannot wait a year. Or a quarter. Or a day. The best time to start fresh is now. Do you have an ad campaign that's grown stale? Now is the time to make it fresh. Are you debating whether it's cost effective to spend thousands, if not tens of thousands, of dollars on a website upgrade to take advantage of new media? It is. Do you have a promotional idea swimming around in your head but you think shooting a video for it is too much of a task? You won't when your competition beats you to the punch. The first out of the gate is usually the one that wins.

You Have The Advantage

Business-to-business companies are more competitive today than ever. You're not only fighting for space against known competitors, but those from other countries who can manufacture your product or reproduce your service for a fraction of the cost. How do you compete? Simple. Make sure your audience knows the difference between them and you. Make certain your message can be heard far and wide in every media channel your customers frequent. Define yourself as the expert in the field and always show them you continue to learn. Your ad campaign, your blog, your website or category-focused site, and your social marketing initiatives – among the many other tools at your disposal – should be a fluid extension of your company. Like that amoeba, you'll need to split, change, and morph in order to grow. Don't be the one who waits to see whether it's prudent to market differently than you have in the past. As author Samuel Johnson states: *"Nothing will ever be attempted, if all possible objections must be first overcome."* Fear is the enemy that persuades you to sit still. Don't. If you're a business owner, you don't need to be told this. You've faced fear because you know risk. If you're a marketing executive who's not sure what to do next, try something outlined here. And whether you're someone who's learning about all of this for the first time or has made a career out of embracing the new, you've got the one thing that the competition cannot take or co-opt from you. The desire to stay a step ahead. Hopefully I've given you some of the tools to help that happen.

A FEW LAST WORDS:

The Marketing Business: How To Survive and Stay Ahead of the Curve

While this chapter may appear to veer away from the focus of this book, particularly in regard to the outlining of B2B strategy, I've written it primarily to discuss something that accompanies your marketing planning:

For Potential Employees: What you should know to help you survive in this industry.

For Marketing Employers: What your employees should take to heart before they come knocking on your door.

Marketing for many is a field people fall into rather than pursue. It is its greatest strength and also its greatest weakness. For every creative soul who wanders through the door of an agency or plants him or herself at the head of the marketing strategy table of a company, there will inevitably be a clash of egos somewhere along the way. It's just the way people in this business are built. For those of you looking to enter this field I've outlined a few tenets to live by that have made me a better executive (and, prior to that, employee). For those looking to hire part of your marketing team, hopefully you'll look for the same qualities in an employee that I find valuable. What follows are a few lessons I've learned in the field that have shaped the way I work and defined the type of people I like to surround myself with.

Lessons for Survival

Some of you who are reading this book will graduate from college, get a great internship or a job right away in a large agency or design firm, and move swiftly up the ladder over the course of decades. You will never have to put together a resume or portfolio because one project will lead to another, one job to the next, one connection to another useful one at a better agency, and so on. You will be promoted from Jr. Account Manager to Sr. Account Manager and Art Director to Group Creative Director in easy succession, and you'll have your name on the agency masthead before you're 30.

Then there's the other 99% of us.

Maybe, once upon a time, the story above was more common in our industry and others. Today, however, it's the story of the very charmed. Most of us, even in optimum circumstances, will not have such an easy career progression. And, besides, luck gets you only part of the way.

As for me, I never had an easy go at this business. Never had positions I didn't have to work my ass off for. Never had a series of generous, trustworthy bosses whose goal was to nurture me as their protégé. Never got anything that didn't come without a boatload of hard work put into it. As a result, my method of moving up the advertising ladder was more akin to Frogger than Pac Man. One step ahead, two back.

The plus side of the school of hard knocks is an innate sense of survival and the development of the skills that foster that. The reason I became one of only a handful of my friends still standing in this industry—where most have either left, been kicked out, withered, or become disillusioned—had more to do with instinct that another bump in the road was always ahead than on an unqualified string of good luck. Longevity in the working world has to be fought for, and the lazy sense of comfort that most people look for in their careers is an illusion, particularly in today's slim job market. You want to succeed despite yourself, despite luck, despite circumstance? This chapter gives yousome tips on what you'll need to do.

Learn Everyone's Job

The first people who go when an agency loses business are the experts. Now, let me explain this one. Every agency needs experts, people who do one thing well, because every agency, either on a regular or irregular day, is a production line. The work filters in from the client to the Account Executive, is strategized by a group, designed by the Creative Director, scripted by a Copywriter, and built in pieces by Production Artists, Flash Designers, Programmers, Animators, Video Producers, etc., etc., etc. There are even successful people right now who have detailed specialties, such as Studio Pro Artists, Photoshop Experts, and PHP Programmers. You get the gist.

The problem with a budget cut, or an outright defection of the client (either because of an unexpected review or an unfortunate mishap, the result of human error) is that tough decisions always have to be made—and those on the losing end are the people whose services are no longer needed on a daily basis. For example, prior to the recent recession, my agency had a solid amount of video work coming from our two biggest clients—nice bits of business that kept my Final Cut Pro editor busy for months on end. After budgets ran dry, cuts were made in marketing (they always cut marketing) and, this time, while the Public Relations, Social Marketing, and General Print Advertising staffs remained, our viral video division suffered. I spent months trying to cull together projects, or bits of projects, to keep my editor busy. He was a good guy, a talented guy, but what became increasingly clear was that we would hit a wall, and I would be forced to cut him as a full-time employee. And that happened, unfortunately.

What would have kept me from doing that? His talents in someplace other than Final Cut Pro. Had he known how to create and implement a social marketing plan or been a Photoshop retouching expert in addition to his chosen job, I could have kept him around until the tide turned. Repositioned him. Now, some of you might say, "Why would he WANT to do anything other than what he loves or was trained at? Isn't an expertise the gateway to success in business?"

In the year 2000, yes. But in the year 2012 and beyond, it's a liability. To survive in today's economy, you need to know other people's jobs. If you are a graphic designer, you need to also be a bit of a Copywriter and an Art Director. If you are a Creative Director, you need to be a Production Artist, Programmer, Account Executive, Copywriter, and Animator. Jobs are fewer today than they've ever been. We compete with other countries now in every industry, even this one, which is usually based on knowledge of local culture and communication and therefore (one would think) immune from competition with those who don't speak English as a first language.

Knowing other people's jobs isn't just a way to keep your own. It's the best way you have to understand HOW a business works and what the owner or manager of that business needs to know to run it.

Here's a story. In 1991, I moved to Los Angeles. At the time, I had an inclination to become a movie director, like millions before and after me, but I had no idea how to get to that position without having several hundred thousand dollars to make a movie. Bear in mind, this was before the HD video revolution. Although some filmmakers, like Nick Gomez and Spike Lee, had created their successes through low-budget black-and-white movies, all of these projects still had to be shot on film, edited on professional equipment in rental houses, and financed with more than lunch money.

Arriving in sunny Culver City (where my brother lived, and with a few scripts in hand), I figured it was just a matter of time, maybe a few months, before I'd be well on my way to directing my first movie.

Unrealistic? Maybe a little bit. It wasn't unheard of.

Anyway, I lacked two primary skills necessary to get closer to that goal. The first was an unwavering level of confidence in myself and the ability to communicate that to others. The second was a persona that compelled people to want to help me or join me. Notice I've purposely left out talent. In my opinion, talent is a given. You can't even get a ticket to ride unless you have it, but that doesn't mean you'll be invited to take a seat.

After having a script option go bad, and flunking out

of my way-out-of-left-field position as an MRI scheduler at UCLA Medical Center, I had to find other work. It was a down economy. I took what I could get. At one point, I was filing film canisters at a warehouse to make ends meet, for a salary that was half of what I had been making back in New York.

Then I got a job in the commercial production department of a promotional ad agency. My boss was a terrifically nice woman named Nancy and, although the pay was even slightly less than the film canister place, it was at least in an industry that I spent a good deal of my early twenties learning. The job was a Jr. Production Coordinator on promotions for the agency's clients, which included Paramount Television and CBS News.

This agency, in the heart of Melrose, was a very L.A place. Everyone dressed well. There were two parking lots for the two private one-floor buildings: the parking lot in front was for anyone with a Mercedes, BMW, or Jaguar; the back lot was for everyone else. I drove a Mazda 323: you know where I had to park. The CEO was reserved (until he yelled) and somewhat intimidating. Within the first few days, I discovered that you don't want to get on the bad side of him or, for that matter, call attention to yourself in any way whatsoever. That was a guarantee you would be cut.

At the time I needed this job. My goal of becoming a director wasn't quite working out. At 26, I even began having an early "mid-life" crisis. One of the first projects I worked on at the company was a commercial for the Lillihammer Olympics. For a while, I toyed with the idea of going to Lake Placid and trying to learn how to luge, the only Olympic event I thought I could possibly learn. For some reason, I felt that since I was approaching 30 and most athletes retire by that age, this would be my last chance at embracing my withering youth. No, I wasn't on drugs.

Anyway, my position had an expiration date. I was a temp. Nancy gave me what she could to keep me busy, but she had another temp who had been there longer than I had, and if the hammer came down, seniority would rule. As it became increasingly clear that I might have to beg for my job back at the film canister company, I found my salvation. It was a small Macintosh SE computer at my desk that was plugged in but doing nothing.

At lunchtime, while everyone was out, I downloaded every program it had onto floppy discs: Aldus Pagemaker, Illustrator, Photoshop 2.0, File Maker. Then I uploaded them to my own Macintosh at home, and I spent my nights sifting through every part of every program. I began with the dropdown on the left, and learned what every function did. On weekends, I spent hours in Barnes & Noble mulling over how-to books to sharpen my skills at these programs—software that my current job didn't require. I couldn't afford to go back to school for any of this—I had neither the time nor the money—so my education would be of my own volition.

Anyhow, I discovered that my services were no longer needed after the next week. That afternoon, I was asked, as I had been many days before, to search for footage from an old commercial. The agency had three huge shelves full of hundreds of ¾" and beta tapes. The amount of hours wasted trying to find anything on these unorganized shelves was monumental. After spending an hour attempting to locate some 1978 promo for KYW in Philadelphia, I had an idea. I ran back to my desk, opened up File Maker, and quickly applied what I had spent nights meticulously learning. Later that afternoon, I made a pitch to Nancy. I had developed a filing mechanism in the software, which I even branded with a name and logo: TapeFinder. I had used the software to create a system that would guarantee finding whatever was needed in seconds rather than hours. She thought it was great, and that extended my job at there for another three months. Survive. That's what I had done. When there was no work at my current position, I created another one. Not only that, but my ingenuity was noted, and that always helps.

So. I had three more months. Not terrible, not great. What happened when my filing system was completed? Well, I had anticipated that and was already working on my next move.

During morning breaks, I had become friends with others at the agency, and I did what I could to understand what everyone did there. In the back building was the creative department. The storyboard artist was an older gentleman named Jim Pearsal. Jim was a crack illustrator who had been in the business for decades, but as a younger man, he had made his bones with movie posters. You can see his illustration work on the posters for *Chinatown* and Charles Bronson's *Breakout*. He had a very particular style that lent itself to storyboard art and, at an agency that did a solid amount of commercial and promotion work, the storyboard art business was booming.

Over time, freelance illustrators came in and out to help Jim. None stayed. Having originally planned on a career as an illustrator or commercial artist, I had always kept up my skills, and I brought my art portfolio wherever I went. After the TapeFinder work dried up, and when Jim was between helpers, I brought in my book. I showed him some storyboards I had done (several nights before) and on the day I would be let go again, I was suddenly reinstated as a Jr. Storyboard Artist.

Once again, my tenacity and survival instinct became my salvation. Then I was offered a real challenge. New promotions had to be delivered as a pitch to Paramount for some of its newer TV shows, which at the time included *Dave's World*, *Murphy Brown*, *Picket Fences*, and others. The powers that be at the agency decided to put its junior people on it, which was me as the storyboard artist and a young guy named Craig as the copywriter. Craig's trajectory was similar to my own, but quite a bit more promising. Craig had also moved out to L.A. with hopes of getting into the movie industry. He also had trouble finding work in a bad economy and found himself at the same temp agency that I had many months before. He came into the place as the copy boy. On Halloween, he decided to create a "Happy Halloween" flyer for the company, which he copied and put on everyone's desk. What he thought would be received with welcome reception ended up pissing off the boss, who wanted him fired. Fortunately for Craig, that didn't happen, thanks to a few sharper minds and his own personality.

Unlike your author, Craig was very social, enthusiastic, and charming. He lit up a room when he entered. As a result, the girls in commercial production loved him, and he earned himself a lot of supporters in the company. When this little incident took place, it pricked up the ears of the company's creative lead. He decided to give Craig an opportunity to do a little copywriting, because the Halloween flyer had been a good sample of that. As a result, Craig was on his way and had gotten, as I had, a second life at a company that very likely would have ejected both of us.

We worked day and night on this pitch. I've not recalled since a time where I've drawn so fast in my entire life. I knew for me to see another day at this company this was a make-or-break situation. As a result, the pitch went well, and a majority of the concepts Craig and I worked on were produced. I was promoted to Jr. Art Director, and I was no longer a temp. I finally had a career in the making.

So, the message here is pretty clear. Your survival in the workforce (and in life, to some degree) depends on your flexibility, your tenacity, your willingness to learn, and the understanding that only luck these days keeps you in a position doing one thing for your entire career. Beyond that, showing an aptitude for other things and the skill of on-the-job learning will get you noticed in a world of employed minions who rarely take the initiative to learn anything they feel they don't need to.

Never Neglect the New Tools of the Trade

"CDs will never catch on. You just can't get the same sound you get from an LP."

"Video will never replace film."

"No one's ever going to buy on the Internet. It's too slow."

Which one of the above statements has proven right? The correct answer is *none of the above*. The correct answer is ALWAYS *none of the above*.

The tools we use for work, play, and daily activity are always changing. The early conversations about their validity have always been consistent. How many times have you heard an old-timer tell you how much better it was in his day than yours? How many of you have parents who steadfastly refuse to learn to use a computer or are just plain intimidated by it?

When those old-timers and parents are retired, well, they can say or do anything they want. But when you work in the advertising business (or many other businesses, for that matter), being stubborn about the tools of your trade is a guarantee that you'll be standing on the unemployment line somewhere down the road.

I bought my first computer, a Magnavox Videowriter, in 1987. My next one was a Macintosh SE in 1991. In between, I learned on whatever computer was in front of me, mostly PCs. By 1994, when I began working at Lois/USA in Manhattan, I was an old hand at Quark, Illustrator, and Photoshop, among other things. I had returned a few months prior from Los Angeles. The ad and design industry was different there.

Computer artwork was the norm. Many agencies may not have been educated enough to know how to use these programs to their full benefit, but all agencies had them on hand.

And so did Lois/USA in 1994. The challenge was that nobody knew what to do with the software at first. There were seven production artists on the board when I arrived ("On the board" meant production artists who did paste-up work). In the days prior to computers, all forms of printed communication in the ad industry were produced by constructing a "collage" of photos, Letraset type, and logo art. Every production artist had a black drawing board, a Sharpie, a razor, and rubber cement that pierced your nostrils and proved to be (for the less-skilled) an absolute mess to use. Really, up until the mid-90s, most agencies still used the same tried-and-true tools they had used for four decades prior.

But whereas scissors remained unchanged in 200 years, most tools have gone through a dramatic transformation as businesses have gotten more advanced and as timely work became a necessity. Especially in the last 10 years with the advent of the Internet and mobile applications, our business has been in a sprint technologically. As a result, many businesses and vendors who have enjoyed lifelong work with modest upgrades never saw the end coming.

Although the Internet has taken over printing as the primary engine for marketing strategies, printers still do exist. But they've become more of a specialty in the last few years than a mainstay. As a result, guys on the board and comp illustrators—those who decided not to learn those newfangled computers—disappeared into the ether. Today, Flash designers are now in jeopardy, as video editing becomes more accessible and streaming media no longer demands the low processing found in the Flash products.

Will these designers cease to exist? No. Not at all. But they will become a specialty. And you know what happens with some specialties, as I explained earlier.

The most pronounced problem I find in both younger and older employees is their slow uptake on the software and skills that are essential to succeed in this business. If you are right out of college today, you better know Photoshop, Illustrator, InDesign, Dreamweaver, Facebook, WordPress, and a little Flash, just to name a few. You also need to know them well. Nothing is more aggravating than hiring someone who claims an expertise in a program, only to find out in short order that he or she isn't advanced enough in it to even *know* what expertise in that program is.

And as far as seasoned employees are concerned—while their experience will always be invaluable—a lack of knowledge of the current tools of the trade, even if you've been a CD many years, won't wash in today's workplace. Most companies look for people who are enthusiastic, always learning, sharp, and forward thinking. If you're a seasoned employee and your software proficiency lists programs that have been out of circulation for a decade, the employer won't to be thinking, "Wow! He's learned a lot of programs," but will instead be saying, "Fontographer?! Does this guy still think grunge is in vogue?"

While working at Lois/USA, I made a point—every weekend—of learning a new program. In 1995, I spent $1,000 of my hard-earned money on the Macromedia Director Suite, which included Director and Extreme 3D. Did I have any current work that needed to be done in these programs? No. In fact, I knew no one who produced multimedia work at the time. But I just had a feeling that it would be to my benefit to learn these for the future. I'd wake up on Saturdays at 5a.m., learned how to produce work like 3D animation, and by 1p.m., have it rendered. (Slow computers back then.)

I didn't simply look through the manual. Instead, I created

a project for myself—in this case, it was a local "virtual neighborhood," kind of a multimedia version of the town illustrations you would find in local businesses anywhere on Long Island—and I moved forward in learning how to create what was in my head. It turned out to be the best way to learn programs for me and, even though those programs are obsolete today, the skills I learned from them are not.

Macromedia Director was a straight line to learning Macromedia Flash. The Lingo language of Director was dramatically more complicated than Action Scripting was in its inception. Consequently, Flash and Director were a direct line to Final Cut Pro, Adobe Premiere, and After Effects. Everything I learned on my own gave me the necessary bump in adapting to more advanced tools that would come up. Even today, as a partner and creative director, I've still found time to master PHP programming, Studio Pro, and other software. As I write this book, I am actively learning HTML5 and testing the waters with Google Plus to see if these new formats and social platforms have legs. Tomorrow, there will be another program to learn and another strategy to integrate.

The marketing business is a business that changes daily, and layabouts will find themselves on the street unless they adapt quickly to change. Change isn't just about learning more, becoming better at your job, and staying up on what's new—a necessity in our world. It is about survival. Those who learn how to do it persevere.

Keep Up On Current Culture

It's easy to get into a rut at work. Particularly today, when the lure of online surfing or Facebooking during business hours is all too present. From time to time, everyone loses steam. Gets burned out. Coasts. For some (and you know who you are), it becomes a habit that defines your tenure. Instead of learning something new or keeping up with the B2B culture of your industry, you convince yourself that the enthusiasm you have for things within your own age range are the only measure of what's important in modern culture.

My parents grew up in the 1930s and '40s. Their musical interests waned somewhere around 1953 with Perry Como and Teresa Brewer. They missed the '60s completely. Barely understood young people of the '70s, and by the '80s, when they were in their 50s, they were completely set in their ways. My dad was lucky enough to have a marketable skill (storyboard art) that was still in demand. He cultivated that skill until he retired at 65. He was one of the lucky ones in this industry.

Today, there is no value in marketing of letting your cultural references remain stagnant. The most innovative work we see comes from many of the younger creative people—and not simply because they are young. What they have that many older employees don't is the desire to suck up new information and culture like it's a milk shake. Granted, they have much more time to do it than we do. Most don't have family obligations or a list of priorities that would choke a horse. On the other hand, they also don't have the perspective an older employee can bring to a campaign when he has the enthusiasm and interest to stay current.

As I discussed in Chapter 3, one of George Lois' great contributions to marketing was not simply in making his MTV campaign feel current (at the time) but also understanding the background of his audience and their cultural underpinnings. His earlier campaign from Maypo oatmeal (with Mickey Mantle and other sports figures crying, "I want my Maypo!" to the camera) was just a small, long suppressed seed in the back of the minds of teenagers and young adults who had been little children when those commercials came out. Lois, very smartly, capitalized on that with the MTV commercials. While the majority of us (I being in that age range) found familiarity with the punk rock graphics and the superstar faces of our rock star heroes, most of us didn't understand why these commercials felt so familiar. We just knew they connected with us. It was the perfect blend of new and old created by a man in his 50s who still understood what it was like to be young.

Let's face it. If you're a bookkeeper at a company that makes writing pads, your need to stay up on who Gotye or Carly Rae Jepsen is—or how to master the art of text messaging—will be limited to how old your children are. But as a marketing person, whether B2B or not, it is the discipline of keeping up with these things that will make the difference as to how valuable you stay in the marketing field later in life.

Accept That You Don't Know It All

Having worked in advertising for quite a few decades, I've had the luxury of being on the cutting edge of a business that has changed dramatically. I've watched printers' fortunes disappear, web programmers become millionaires, and mighty agencies that were once the toast of Madison Avenue shrink and dissolve with little fanfare.

My position—as an Art Director, then a Creative Director and Agency Partner—has transitioned from drawing illustrations for commercial storyboards to performing as a company head whose day involves attending strategy meetings, tinkering with PHP code, editing in Final Cut Pro, texting with outside vendors to meet product deadlines, participating in teleconferences, implementing social marketing campaigns, and retouching in Photoshop so delicately as to be called an art.

In contrast, I've also observed some friends of mine—teachers, lawyers, accountants, and social workers—whose careers and job duties haven't really changed all that much over the same time period. Sure, they use the Internet as teaching tools and QuickBooks for their clients' taxes. They keep in touch through mobile applications and participate in webinars, but, unlike me, they've never had to reassess and relearn the essence of what they do.

Where successful businesses take the form of amoebas, the marketing industry in the last 20 years has always been a multi-celled organism in constant flux. It is not an industry where certainty rules, like law, for example. We know from past successes what might work for our clients, but as new marketing channels and ways of communicating open up daily, our ability to determine without question what will win and lose in a B2B market is itself questionable.

Marketing professionals need to be flexible. Just as too many large advertising agencies had been slow on the uptake of digital marketing, too many creative people make rash judgments on what their agencies are and are not.

If you wish to thrive in this industry, the path is pretty clear. You must be innovative by nature. You should have the curiosity to learn new things all the time—and you need a mechanical mind to put it all together. It is no longer viable (for longevity anyway) to be someone who looks at a creative print ad as nirvana and the world of interactive marketing and social media as annoying fads. Will the social marketing push wither in the upcoming future? Yes and no. Certainly, the current fever for everything social (despite the large percentage of it being "added value" as opposed to lead generation) will dissipate, and more direct methods of lead generation through such media will be more clearly defined. We are still in the early frontiers of this trend.

But just as electronic media has outpaced and flattened

print media in the last decade, digital marketing may well do the same. A whole new world of mobile applications, the potential for 3D interactive video material (where customers can see products three dimensionally on their computers and virtually move them), and a newer generation of users that spends more time communicating through devices rather than physical interaction guarantee the longevity of these strategies in the long term.

The only thing that stands between those who will succeed in this space and those who won't is the willingness to assume that there is always more to learn, always new methods of engagement to discover, and an almost-constant forward motion of technology that will make our futuristic-like present day look quaint by comparison a few short years from now.

High-School Politics Are Real-World Politics

Remember that moment you graduated from high school? You thought, from this moment on, everything would be different. People would act like adults. Arguments would be resolved quickly and thoughtfully. Life in "the real world" would be a dramatic difference from everything you knew before. If you went to college, well, that was a step in the right direction for that mindset. Depending on the school, your high school status was suddenly equalized. Nobody knew you, so you had the opportunity to reinvent yourself, and you did.

Now, all that good will, studious equality, and organization would be put to the test as you prepare yourself for what would come next.

If you're like most of us, you found yourself either bemused or shocked at how familiar the real world was from the world you couldn't wait to leave. The working world is not easy. If you're lucky, you find yourself in a company where your value

value is based on your abilities and your work. Most of the time, however, companies take on the personalities of their leader and, if their leader acts like a mischievous frat boy, your company has an element of that in its culture. If he or she is two-faced, that uncertainty will affect everyone else in the company. If your leader is deceptive and political, watch out. That will be 60% of your workweek trying to maneuver in and out of little squabbles and posturing.

Despite what you hear, there is little truth to the theory that politics destroy all companies. When it does happen, it's rare. In reality, politics in most companies is heard but not seen. It's particularly prominent in large companies that have been around for some time.

I've worked for large and small outfits. My best experience was with Lois/USA, where the politics may only have been prevalent for the top brass. The rest of the company got along terrifically, and the boss was very loyal. For some time, I was a full-time freelancer there. I was paid very well. By the end of the first year, however, the second partner brought in a "cleaner"— a gentleman hired to cut costs, rearrange structure and, apparently, help the company to function better. The problem with this cleaner was his arrogance at "knowing" how a company he hadn't been involved in for more than a week should work and his ignorance at what did, and has worked, for decades.

Being freelance, I was one of the first on his radar. He recommended I be let go. Fortunately for me, and thanks to the culture of the company (and its leader), I was untouchable. George, as I said, was very loyal to his team. Some of the guys working for him had been there for more than 20 years. My creative director, Dennis Mazzella, defended my position and George backed him up. The result of the conversation with the cleaner was that he was no longer welcome in the creative department and was required to look elsewhere for changes. Having had only bad experiences at companies up to that point, I was grateful that there were positive experiences to be had, and it kept me in a business that I might otherwise have left if that situation had gone south.

In any event, the cleaner decided to use another tactic. He enacted a rule that all company employees had to be on staff. As a result, I was brought on staff for a salary that was half of what I was making as a freelancer. Within a month, I decided I couldn't continue and wrote my resignation letter.

One week after I resigned, I was hired back—as a freelancer at a my earlier salary. The team that supported me had done a runaround with the cleaner and once again reinforced my belief that not all companies are political nightmares.

On the other end of the spectrum, my worst experience came from a company that was frighteningly political. The problem there was the company leader. She was bipolar, pitted people against each other to test their loyalty, and treated most of her employees as flavors of the month. Five months in, after a few rounds of layoffs (some unnecessary), I was suddenly one of the senior people at the company. It was not to last. When faced with a situation like this, it's best to recognize what you're involved in and understand that this will be a short-term position. If the money's right and the job is a benefit to your future (or your portfolio), you tolerate it as long as you see fit—or, better yet, walk away if you can.

In short, there is no nirvana unless you are fundamental to creating the company yourself. There are dozens of examples of out-of-the-box work cultures out there (Google, whose internal slogan is "Do no harm," comes to mind) that are built out of optimism and the desire to put aside childish games as working adults. The best you can do is know your place in this process, whether it's a world that works for you or not, and know that there is always a better fit for you out there if you have the courage to look for it.

Paying Your Dues Doesn't End On Your Time Clock

Prior to the economic troubles of the last half a decade, my last employer hired a lot of interns who lacked motivation, and we interviewed more than can be counted that just plain felt the world owed them something. Maybe they were raised by parents who had it far too easy or who pampered their kids too much, or maybe someone told them they were the center of the universe and shouldn't ever accept less than they want, but some of the latest crop of new recruits need attitude readjustments.

Paying your dues isn't an incubation period. It is a way of doing business that is also in place for new employees. If you want to distinguish yourself in the workplace today, you need to really step it up. The first priority shouldn't be getting a particular salary so you can lease that Mercedes you can't afford. It should be to find out everything you can about your position and work your ass off to make yourself invaluable. The benefit younger workers have is their unlimited reservoir of free time. This time should not be wasted on Facebook chatting with friends about your awesome dinner. It should be used to build portfolios, working overtime, and being willing to make yourself available for extra projects.

Doctors enter into residency not only because hospitals need the cost-effective help. They are put through this sometimes grueling process to weed out the candidates who are not fit for this kind of work and moving up the ones who are. The bar exam is similar. Lawyers cannot practice unless they pass, and the testing is not easy, as John Kennedy Jr. discovered when he found himself taking it three times.

While I was Creative Director for Gem Group, I once hired a guy who had only worked in large ad agencies. We were a mid-sized agency with a creative department of 14. For the month that he was there, he spent most of the time complaining that his previous agencies hadn't required him to work on so many different projects at once or use so many different types of programs. As we discovered, he was fluent only in QuarkXPress, despite a resume that touted Photoshop, Illustrator, and other programs. His inability to adapt to our pace (which was fast, precise, and required a variety of skills in print and online) eventually forced me to pull the plug on him. He had never been fired before and really wanted to know why. I explained it to him in detail, and he was floored. He had no idea that there was a world out there beyond the structure of larger ad firms, where most designers were given one skill to hone, because creative departments were huge. I wonder how well he has fared in recent years, where even the larger outfits have pared down to the bare essentials with their workers. I hope he learned the lesson that the world of work is vast and varied—and that believing your way is the only way doesn't always work in places where sacrifice is necessary to learn your job well for today and the future.

Be Willing to Fail: You Might Learn Something

When I was younger, I was fired so many times I stopped counting. Sometimes it was for stupid things, like not making the salad for the next morning's rush at International House of Pancakes when I was a teenager. Another time, it was the result of making too sharp a turn in a company minivan and bouncing two-wheels-at-a-time down a circular off-ramp, as our clients, in the back seat, shrieked in horror. (I still kept my job for two days after that one.) Despite all the evidence that

I was either ill-equipped or incompetent at what I was doing, I always maintained the confidence that there was something out there that I could do well. In my case, it was creative work for advertising (or so I'd like to think).

Nonetheless, failure is as much a given in the world of business as success. You cannot find the right equation for any solution without going through a few rough drafts and failed calculations beforehand.

Some failure is good. Most successful entrepreneurs know this. Failure means success is right around the corner. It does not mean you are forever a bad bet in the business world, unless you've learned nothing from your failures.

My failures have been my greatest teacher. Having been fired a few times, I've never since taken for granted any position I've had that I've wanted. I've never lost an opportunity to learn more than what was put in front of me. At any turn, I've always felt my position in life was threatened. As a result, I've never been complacent and always on alert. If you learn these skills without having to fail many times beforehand, you'll be better off in the long run.

We Are All Frauds at What We Do

Sometimes I wear a suit to new business meetings to appear "professional." I am frequently acknowledged to be the smartest guy in the room. I can expound on issues of marketing, advertising, design, strategy, online interactivity, what makes good copy, what does and doesn't work, and so on and so on.

Still, no matter what I say, how certain I am that it's true, how smart I seem to appear, or how much my words actually mean to others, I am and will always be a fraud. And I'm okay with that.

You see, we are all frauds.

Do you still view yourself as a teenager playing dress-up and pretending to be business big shots? Have you passed the bar with flying colors and still, in quiet moments, wonder how anyone can believe you're their lawyer? How many U.S. presidents have turned a corner in the oval office and, just for a moment, wondered who put them in charge and how crazy those people must have been?

In my mind, seeing oneself as a fraud is what makes a good businessperson great. Knowing that you are not perfect and can improve—and seeing that potential and human frailty in others—can bond you to your employees and clients better. Hopefully, they can have the same insight as you. By allowing yourself to be viewed as imperfect, maybe a little flaky (but not too flaky) or awkward sometimes results in the opposite response that kind of openness might have played out in high school, when everyone was insecure and trying to be invisible. Most people who get up in years recognize that someone's humanity, not their slickness, is where the honesty resides.

Up until the age of 38 (when it miraculously became controllable), I suffered through a mild version of Tourette's Syndrome. I was never known to scream obscenities or anything quite so pronounced, mostly, I just twitched. I was terribly self-conscious. Had to get in a few fights in high school just to mute a few kids who couldn't help but make fun of me. Nonetheless, I looked upon it as more of an annoyance I needed to conquer than anything else. I still dated, had friends, succeeded in the working world despite it, got married, had two beautiful kids and came to terms with the fact that I am imperfect, can't fix it, and will have to work with it. I've seen others like me across the table at meetings with the same affliction. While any of us who've had it can tell you a bout of it has little to do with our confidence or lack thereof, it does seem to the outsider that we are not as calm, cool or collected as we may actually be. More than anyone else, we have a tougher time hiding from the world that we are not our facades.

But, you see, perceiving yourself as a fraud is liberating. You no longer have to put on a front and present yourself as a rigid, perfectly creased businessperson, particularly if you are from an ad agency. Your personality is what is of value there because open people help feed creativity in an agency.

And besides, the more you know that everyone else in the room also views themselves as frauds, the more comfortable you can be selling them on ideas you're passionate about rather than questioning whether your outfit or your posture is going to lose the account for you.

Notes:

Chapter 1

1.   "In 2011, Google surveyed 600 business-to-business marketing professionals…", B2B Marketing Guide 2011 Edition, http://blog.kissmetrics.com/2011-b2b-marketing-guide/

2.   "This perception is changing" http://www.carolinabannerexchange.com/banner-ad-comeback.htm

3.   "No industry embodies the dramatic change our digital and social landscape has brought us more than the music industry." http://www.digitalmusicnews.com/stories/081611thirty

4.   "One of the smartest moves Apple made early in their history was to partner with companies that produced software for the publishing and design businesses." http://desktop-pub.about.com/cs/beginners/f/when_dtp.htm

5.   "According to The American Marketing Association (AMA) branding is defined as a "name, term, sign, symbol or design, or a combination of them intended to identify the goods and services of one seller or group of sellers and to differentiate them from those of other sellers." http://chicagoama.org/behind-branding-scenes

6.   http://www.b2bento.com/2011/06/but-we-are-not-selling-coca-cola-says-the-ceo/

7.   http://www.business.com/b2bmarketing/category/b2b-lead-gen

8.   "According to Boise, the goals of the promotion were as follows:", "*Boise Cascade Office Products Promotion Wins National Marketing Award Apr 11, 2000*", http://officemax.mediaroom.com/index.php?s=43&item=166

9.   "The amateur aesthetic can be traced all the way back to the release of two independent films - 1959's Shadows by John Cassavetes and the French film, Breathless, by Jean-Luc Godard the following year."
a) "John Cassavetes' startling directorial debut changed American movies forever." Slate, Nov. 11, 2009, http://www.slate.com/articles/arts/dvdextras/2009/11/shadows.html
b) "*Why Breathless Still Matters, 50 Years Later*", Moviefone, May 27th 2010, http://blog.moviefone.com/2010/05/27/breathless-50th-anniversary-re-release

10.   "*What's the Big Idea?*", Lois, George, Doubleday 1991, Pg. 3-4

11.   "Their message was that this new company had its own airline and, therefore, didn't get bogged down with the time-consuming task of moving packages from one commercial flight to another." http://www.youtube.com/watch?v=mX42MK4IfSY&feature=autoplay&list=PL1D705AE52D11D7E2&lf=results_video&playnext=2

Chapter 2

12. UPS White Board Ads, http://www.slate.com/articles/business/ad_report_card/2007/04/back_to_the_drawing_board.html, http://thebuzzbubble.com/e07-pt-2-andy-azula-talks-about-the-making-of-the-ups-whiteboard-campaign.html

13. "*Social Works*" by Fletcher, Heather, Target Marketing, February 2010 http://www.targetmarketingmag.com/article/games-networks-blogs-part-ibm-software-groups-strategy/1

14. "*Content Rules*" by Handly, Ann & Chapman, C.C., John Wiley & Sons, ©2011

15. Seth Godin on Blogging, Business Books, and Creating Content that Matters, http://www.copyblogger.com/seth-godin-podcast/

16. http://en.wikipedia.org/wiki/Engadget

17. Boston.com "*Ready for her close-ups*", by Raman, Sheela, August 13, 2005, http://www.boston.com/news/globe/living/articles/2005/08/13/ready_for_her_close_ups/?page=full

Chapter 3

18. 101Cliches.com

19. David Meerman Scott, Social Media Club, Amsterdam http://www.youtube.com/watch?v=pzhfVXprMls

Chapter 4

20. "*Your Marketing Plan*" by Duncan, Apryl, http://advertising.about.com/od/planning/a/marketingplan.htm

21. "*Online Advertising Market Poised To Grow In 2011*" by eMarketer, http://www.emar-keter.com/PressRelease.aspx?R=1008432

22. "*Harnessing Mobility – Going Mobile with Oracle Apps*" by Bharat, Brijesh, http://www.slideshare.net/brijeshbharat/harness-mobility-go-mobile-on-oracle-apps

23. http://competipedia.com/Groundswell.aspx

24. http://blog.prnewswire.com/2011/09/06/curating-content-on-twitter-for-thought-leadership/

25. http://windmillnetworking.com/2011/04/14/twitter-b2b-marketing-case-studies/

26. "*Google Plus Pages For Businesses Continue To Demonstrate SEO Benefits*" by Isca, Frank, Business2Community.com, December 21, 2011, http://www.business2community.com/google-plus/google-plus-pages-for-businesses-continue-to-demonstrate-seo-benefits-0110305

Chapter 5

27. Matt Cutts, GoogleWebmasterHelp, YouTube, http://www.youtube.com/watch?v=FPBACTS-tyg

28. Extron.com

29. *"Responsive Web Design"* by Marcotte, Ethan, A List Apart, May 25, 2010, http://www.alistapart.com/articles/responsive-web-design/

Chapter 7

30. *"3 Hard Lessons to Learn From Penguin: Be Relevant, Be Balanced, Keep it Real"*, http://searchenginewatch.com/article/2180059/3-Hard-Lessons-to-Learn-From-Penguin-Be-Relevant-Be-Balanced-Keep-it-Real

31. *"Escaping the Wrath of Google Penguin"*, http://www.northcutt.com/blog/2012/04/escaping-wrath-of-google-penguin/

32. *"The Gold in Social Customer Service"*, http://www.forbes.com/sites/christinecrandell/2011/10/08/the-gold-in-social-customer-service/

33. *"Shattering the Myth about Keyword Density Formula"*, http://www.shoutmeloud.com/urban-legends-shattering-the-myth-about-keyword-density.html

Chapter 9

34. *"The Greatest Fast Food Gimmick Ever"*, http://awesdumb.com/index.php?option=com_content&view=article&id=11:the-greatest-fast-food-gimmick-ever&catid=3:rants&Itemid=4

35. *"Have Trade magazines got a shelf life?"* By Dowell, Ben, The Guardian, April 24, 2011, http://www.guardian.co.uk/media/2011/apr/25/trade-magazines-online-only

36. *"Creative Keys To Trade Show Success: Before the Show"* by Trani, Amber, November 2, 2011, https://www.map-dynamics.com/blog/2312/Creative_Keys_to_Trade_Show_Success%3A_Before_the_Event.html

37. *"Trade Show Planning: Your Roadmap To Success"*, Trade-ShowAdvisor.com, http://www.trade-show-advisor.com/trade-show-planning.html

38. *"Seth Godin's Advice For Creating Remarkable Content"* by Hubspot Blog, March 24, 2011, http://blog.onlinemarketingconnect.com/hubspot/2011/03/seth-godins-advice-for-creating-remarkable-content/

39. *"11 Simple Steps To A Powerful Webinar"*, http://www.speakerscommunity.com/blog/2008/01/13/11-simple-steps-to-a-powerful-webinar/

40.   "*CerviLenz – A B2B Social Media Case Study*" by Miller, Patrick, http://my.bkv.com/blog/comments/cervilenz-a-b2b-social-media-case-study/

41.   "*UPS One Of The Best Examples Of B2B Social Media*", October 11, 2011, http://www.ceekue.com/ups-one-of-the-best-examples-of-b2b-social-media/

42.   "*UPS Launches Social Media Marketing Campaign*" by Skepys, Brian, September 14, 2010, Social Media Influence, http://socialmediainfluence.com/2010/09/14/ups-launches-a-b2b-social-marketing-campaign/

43.   "Case Study: Shipserv", courtesy Haakon Jenson (http://haakonjensen.no/2010/06/case-study-shipserv/)

44.   "Get Bold Using Social Media to Create a New Type of Social Business" by Carter, Sandy, IBM Press 2012, http://my.safaribooksonline.com/9780132618427/ch04sec1lev7?reader=html&imagepage=

Index:

Bill Blaney and members of his company are available for marketing consultations and speaking engagements.

For more information, please call **917-686-5704** or email us at **info@b2bmarketingneeds.com**

29721457R00140

Made in the USA
San Bernardino, CA
26 January 2016